DICKENS'S
GREAT EXPECTATIONS

CONTINUUM READER'S GUIDES

William Blake's Poetry – Jonathan Roberts

Achebe's Things Fall Apart – Ode Ogede

Conrad's Heart of Darkness – Allan Simmons

Fitzgerald's The Great Gatsby – Nicolas Tredell

Sylvia Plath's Poetry – Linda Wagner-Martin

DICKENS'S
GREAT EXPECTATIONS

A Reader's Guide

IAN BRINTON

continuum

Continuum International Publishing Group
The Tower Building
11 York Road
London
SE1 7NX

80 Maiden Lane
Suite 704
New York
NY 10038

British Library Cataloguing-in-Publication Data
A catalogue record for this book is available from the British Library.

ISBN – 10: 0 8264 8857 9 (hardback)
          0 8264 8858 7 (paperback)
ISBN – 13: 978 08264 8857 2 (hardback)
          978 08264 8858 9 (paperback)

Library of Congress Cataloging-in-Publication Data
A catalog record for this book is available from the Library of Congress.

Typeset by Servis Filmsetting Ltd, Manchester
Printed and bound in Great Britain by MPG Books Ltd, Bodmin, Cornwall

CONTENTS

NOTES ON SOURCES

Full publication details for all works cited can be found in the final chapter, 'Works Cited and Further Reading'. After an initial list of editions of *Great Expectations* and other Dickens works, this chapter is arranged thematically in line with Chapters 1–5.

All quotations from *Great Expectations* are from the Penguin Classics edition, introduced by David Trotter and edited by Charlotte Mitchell (2003).

CHAPTER 1

CONTEXTS

Born in Portsmouth on 7 February 1812, the most significant years of Charles Dickens's early life were spent in London and in north Kent. The family had moved to London in 1815 so that the novelist's father, John Dickens, could take up his duties as a clerk in the Navy Pay Office at Somerset House. In 1817 they moved to the dockyard town of Chatham near Rochester and it was whilst living in Chatham that Charles first came across Gad's Hill Place, a house which he was later to own. In an 1857 letter to John Forster, he commented that the house 'has always had a curious interest for me, because, when I was a small boy down in these parts, I thought it the most beautiful house . . . ever seen. And my poor father used to bring me to look at it, and used to say that if I ever grew up to be a clever man, perhaps I might own that house, or such another house. In remembrance of which, I have always in passing, looked to see if it was to be sold or let; and it has never been to me like any other house, and it has never changed at all' (*Letters of Charles Dickens: Volume 8*, pp. 265–6). The haunting seriousness of the story is emphasized by its inclusion in the article, 'Travelling Abroad' from *All the Year Round*, 7 April 1860 (*Dickens' Journalism, vol. 4*). The central importance of these early years in Chatham is highlighted by Michael Allen in *Charles Dickens' Childhood*:

> At Chatham the genteel way of life in an otherwise violent and bawdy town formed Charles' view of his family's position in the community and his own expectations from life: here John Dickens enjoyed his best ever income, the family employed two servants and Charles thrived on success and encouragement at

school, visits to the theatre, books to read, parties to go to, friends to play with.

(p. 9)

However, the financial difficulties, aggravated by his own profligacy, which were to plague John Dickens's life prompted a change of house in Chatham in 1821 and then a move to more narrow accommodation in Camden Town, London in 1822. The schooling which Dickens had begun earlier that year was discontinued, and in another letter to Forster he made clear the significance of the loss: 'As I thought in the little back garret in Bayham Street, of all I had lost in losing Chatham, what would I have given, if I had had anything to give, to be sent back to any other school, to have been taught anything anywhere!' (Forster, p. 11). A further move in 1823, to Gower Street, was swiftly followed by Dickens being sent to work in Warren's Blacking warehouse at Hungerford Stairs in order to ease the financial burdens of the household, and the lasting stain of this experience is registered in his manuscript fragments of autobiography, which he sent to Forster in 1847:

It is wonderful to me how I could have been so easily cast away at such an age. It is wonderful to me, that, even after my descent into the poor little drudge I had been since we came to London, no one had compassion enough on me – a child of singular abilities, quick, eager, delicate, and soon hurt, bodily or mentally – to suggest that something might have been spared, as certainly it might have been, to place me at any common school.

His description of the place provides a startling contrast with the aspiration to live in Gad's Hill Place:

The blacking warehouse was the last house on the left-hand side of the way at old Hungerford Stairs. It was a crazy, tumbledown old house, abutting of course on the river, and literally overrun with rats. Its wainscotted rooms and its rotten floors and staircase, and the old grey rats swarming down in the cellars, and the sound of their squeaking and scuffling coming up the stairs at all times, and the dirt and decay of the place rise up visibly before me as if I were there again.

He had acquired the nickname 'the young gentleman' while working with Bob Fagin and others, and commented in the autobiographical sketch that

> No words can express the secret agony of my soul as I sunk into this companionship; compared these everyday associates with those of my happier childhood; and felt my early hopes of growing up to be a learned and distinguished man, crushed in my breast. The deep remembrance of the sense I had of being utterly neglected and hopeless; of the shame I felt in my position; of the misery it was to my young heart to believe that, day by day, what I had learned, and thought, and delighted in, and raised my fancy and my emulation up by, was passing away from me, never to be brought back any more; cannot be written.
>
> (Forster, pp. 17–19)

The nostalgic quality which haunts the opening pages of *Great Expectations*, accompanied by a sense of both fear and loss, registers the way in which Dickens felt about his early life before the shattering experience of imprisonment in the blacking warehouse. The deeply felt nature of the shame of loss lies beneath the secrecy Dickens felt about the incident: 'That I suffered in secret, and that I suffered exquisitely, no one ever knew but I' (Forster, p. 21). This secrecy and sense of shabby shame recur in Pip's feelings upon his first visit to Satis House, in chapter 8 of the novel, when he is 'so humiliated, hurt, spurned, offended, angry, sorry' and the fragments of autobiographical writing remained unpublished until Forster's posthumous biography appeared between 1872 and 1874.

In early 1824 John Dickens was arrested for debt and incarcerated in the Marshalsea Prison near the Borough, and the effects of the debt were felt in the home as most of the furniture was pawned before the family moved into the prison to remain together. Dickens, lodging nearby, was a regular visitor to the prison, dividing his time between there and the blacking warehouse. On his father's release later that year, a family altercation led to the 12-year-old Charles ceasing work at the blacking warehouse, which had now moved to more public premises in Covent Garden. However, his mother, with no awareness of the depths of her son's feelings, was prepared to heal over the rift so that he could resume his employment. The continuing preoccupation which Dickens felt with this betrayal became instrumental to the underlying theme of *Dombey and Son*, where the parent has no understanding of the needs of the child. Referring to his mother's willingness for him to return to the blacking warehouse which had been a world of nightmare to him, Dickens wrote: 'I never afterwards forgot, I never shall forget, I never can forget, that my mother was warm for my being sent back' (Forster, p. 26). In the 1848 Christmas Book, *The Haunted Man*, the spectral double of Redlaw comments 'My parents at the best, were of that sort whose care soon ends, and whose duty is soon done; who cast their offspring loose, early, as birds do theirs; and, if they do well, claim the credit; and, if ill, the pity' (*Christmas Books*, p. 332). However, his father intervened and Dickens resumed his education as a day-pupil at Wellington House Academy in Hampstead Road and 'the well-turned-out lad with the proud head and the uncontrollable laughter' tried to escape from 'the shabby labouring hind he was trying to forget'.

After joining the solicitors firm of Ellis & Blackmore in May 1827 and learning shorthand, Dickens became a freelance reporter in Doctors' Commons and then a parliamentary reporter in March 1832. In 1829 he had met and fallen in love with Maria Beadnell and later recorded that 'all delight lay in being with her and all misery, though delicious misery lit with visions, in being separated from her' (Johnson, vol. 1, p. 72). However, her father disapproved of the connection, and after she had been sent away to Paris to complete her education she returned more distant and cold. In 'Birthday Celebrations', published in *All the Year Round*, 6 June 1863, there may well be a reference to the 21st-birthday party which sealed the end of the relationship, since the letters sent to Maria Beadnell in March 1833 confirm that her painful rejection of his suit took place at this time. In the article, writing as 'The Uncommercial Traveller', Dickens comments that 'in the crumby part of the night when wine glasses were to be found in unexpected spots, I spoke to Her – spoke out to Her' (*Dickens' Journalism, vol. 4*). She, however, 'scorched' his brain by referring to him as a 'Boy', a disdainful comment which re-emerges in Estella's reference to Pip as 'a common labouring-boy' in chapter 8 of *Great Expectations*. Edgar Johnson suggests that 'All the rest of his emotional life he lay under the shadow of this lost love, which in its darkest places merges with the shadow cast by the spiked wall of the Marshalsea and the imprisoning shades of the blacking warehouse' (Johnson, vol. 1, p. 83).

Having started his first contributions to the *Monthly Magazine* in 1832 he adopted the pen-name Boz in August 1833 and started writing for the *Morning Chronicle*. In 1835 Dickens met Catherine Hogarth, whose father was editor of the *Evening Chronicle*, which published 20 of the Boz sketches over the following seven months. This in turn led to the suggestion that the articles should be collected into a book, illustrated by George Cruikshank, to be published as *Sketches by Boz*. It was to include 'A Visit to Newgate', which the *Chronicle*'s editor suggested would 'make' any book and which, after publication, was likened to Victor Hugo's *Dernier Jour d'un Condamné*. The favourable reception of the *Sketches*, subtitled 'Illustrative of Everyday Life and Everyday People', immediately led to a proposal from Chapman and Hall to contribute to their 'Library of Fiction' and write the text to accompany a series of illustrations by the comic sporting artist, Robert Seymour, based on the comic perils and mishaps befalling the 'Nimrod Club' of cockneys who set themselves up as sporting experts. Interestingly, Henry Mayhew had been already approached by Seymour for the task but he had turned it down, and when Dickens agreed to the proposal in February 1836 it was the beginning of what became the monthly publication of *The Pickwick Papers*.

With an increased income brought in through this commission, Dickens and Catherine Hogarth married, and Edgar Johnson suggests that 'he had an ideal picture in his imagination of what marriage should be like, a sweet and brightly coloured domesticity in which at the end of his day's work he would turn for happiness to the fond looks and gentle ways of his wife' (Johnson, vol. 1, p. 130). In contrast to this vision, Dickens never told his wife of the hidden shame of working in the blacking warehouse which had left such a stain upon his early years, nor would she have been aware of the shadows cast by the walls of the Marshalsea on the growing boy. With such a constraint upon their intimacy it was perhaps unfortunate that they set up household within the confines of three rooms and accompanied by Catherine's younger sister, Mary, whom Dickens surrounded with imaginative idealization so that she became 'the grace and life of our home' (*ibid.*).

The immense success of the monthly instalments of *Pickwick* led to an invitation in August 1836 to edit Bentley's *Miscellany*, and George Cruikshank was employed to illustrate a new novel in 24 instalments which appeared there between January 1837 and April 1839. Its title, *The Adventures of Oliver Twist, or the Parish Boy's Progress*, marked it out as unusual in its depiction of the importance of the life of a child and the inescapable effects of upbringing on a growing boy. While *The Pickwick Papers* had already introduced readers to the serious dimension of the debtors' prison and the outrageous bullying injustice of Sergeant Buzfuz, the nightmare experience of Warren's Blacking Warehouse informs Fagin's squalid den. The effect of the Poor Law Amendment Act of 1834, which created 600 unions of parishes managed by boards of guardians elected by ratepayers, was felt in the harsh exercise of power in the workhouses which provided subsistence for paupers. The lifelong fascination with prisons which haunted Dickens led him to use his Newgate visit from the *Sketches*, where his concentration was upon a condemned man in his cell and his 'fears of death', which 'amount almost to madness'.

With the increased financial security provided by the success of his writing, Dickens took out a three-year lease on a pleasant 12-room dwelling in Doughty Street, London. However, after only one month there, Mary, who sympathized with all Dickens's thoughts and feelings 'more than anyone I knew ever did or will', suddenly died. The ring that he slipped from her finger as she expired in his arms was to remain on his hand until his own death some 43 years later.

In early 1838, Dickens and Hablôt K. Browne (Phiz), the illustrator with whom he had worked on *Pickwick* after the unexpected suicide of Robert Seymour, took a journey to Yorkshire in order to research material about schools in preparation for a monthly publication for Chapman and Hall, *The Life and Adventures of Nicholas Nickleby*. Schools in Yorkshire were notorious for negligence and cruelty as was evidenced by the trial of William Shaw, who ran an academy at Bowes near Greta Bridge where it transpired that the boys were given maggoty food and slept five to a bed. The graveyard at Bowes boasts the graves of 25 boys from 7 to 18 who died there between 1810 and 1824. *Nicholas Nickleby* follows the 'life and adventures' pattern of eighteenth-century picaresque fiction and is an example of *bildungsroman* in that it recounts the development of the individual from childhood to maturity up to the point when the hero recognises his place in the world. However, as yet, the writing does not have the sophistication of either *David Copperfield* or *Great Expectations*.

Between the spring of 1840 and December 1841, Dickens edited a weekly journal, *Master Humphrey's Clock*, which saw the publication of both *The Old Curiosity Shop* and *Barnaby Rudge*. The former centres around the fantastic nineteenth-century dream of speculation leading to riches and the magical transformation of ordinary people into ladies and gentleman. The fairy-tale aspects of this dream are contrasted with the sordid gambling mania of Little Nell's grandfather and the debt-ridden constraints suffered by Dick Swiveller who finds that 'The roads are closing so fast in every direction, that in about a month's time, unless my aunt sends me a remittance, I shall have to go three or four miles out of town to get over the way' (*The Old Curiosity Shop*, p. 60). The most striking pages in *Barnaby Rudge* describe the burning down of Newgate and they register the destruction of the dark symbol of imprisonment which had branded his own memories of childhood.

To rest from the enormous burden of the weekly writing commitments, Dickens took Catherine to America for most of 1842, and *American Notes for General Circulation* catalogues his impressions of that journey. Despite the enormous success of much of the expedition there was a sour tone to the disagreements about international copyright and the descriptions of the Tombs prison in New York and the 'solitary prison' of Philadelphia darken the shining dream of the New World. Even so, the book of impressions sold three thousand copies in its first week and four large editions before the end of 1842. Forster noted that Dickens 'returned from America with wider views than when he started, and with more maturity of mind' and in his opinion 'it was the turning point of his career' (Forster, p. 193). This judgement is borne out by the writing in monthly parts of *Martin Chuzzlewit*, a novel which centres around selfishness. The sales of the new novel were poor and this may well reflect the transition in the writing from affectionate comedy, which had tempered the most bitter satire in earlier work, to what Edgar Johnson calls 'a grimmer gaze for human shortcomings' (Johnson, vol. 1, p. 470). The characters of Pecksniff and Mrs Gamp represent a social order which professes moral standards while being inextricably bound up with sordid material ends: respectability with its eye to the main chance for self-promotion. This relationship between materialism, monetary greed and selfishness dominates the short story which Dickens wrote during the autumn and winter of 1843, *A Christmas Carol*.

Returning to London in the summer of 1845 Dickens was preoccupied with the idea of setting up as editor of a new daily paper, to be called *Daily News*. Not only would the regular income be welcome, but the paper could also become a voice to highlight the young novelist's views of the corruption and inhumanity of the social scene, and trumpet the need for radical reforms. In January 1846, amid parliamentary confusion about the resignation of Peel over the issue of the repealing of the Corn Laws, the first edition was printed advocating 'Principles of Progress and Improvement'. However, handing over the editorship to Forster in February, Dickens was now contemplating another novel and he travelled with the family to Lausanne where he began *Dombey and Son*. Moving from the old stagecoach days which had dominated his fiction so far, an England that was fast changing, this new novel was firmly based in the age of railway travel, squalid suburbs and the financial risks of speculation. Published in 20 monthly parts, the figure of Dombey was a departure from the respectable business-man as he had appeared in Dickens's earlier fiction. The stiff propriety and frigid manners of a man whose relations with the surrounding world are reduced to matters of monetary power mark this character as the unbending epitome of pride. Interestingly, an analysis of the chronology of *Great Expectations* reveals that its action spans the period between 1812 and 1829, the Regency period of the Napoleonic wars and the new world of steam-powered railway locomotives that heralded a growth of a flourishing economy, and increased investment capital which led to the development of a vast railway network. *Dombey and Son* was a financial triumph, selling 34,000 copies by June 1848 (in contrast with Thackeray's *Vanity Fair* which at the same time was selling 5,000 copies), and any embarrassments which Dickens may have had with money were ended.

The Personal History of David Copperfield, published in monthly parts between May 1849 and November 1850, was, like *Great Expectations*, written in the first person and Johnson comments: 'Few novelists have ever captured more poignantly the feeling of childhood, the brightness and magic and terror of the world as seen through the eyes of a child and coloured by his dawning emotions' (Johnson, vol. 2, p. 677).

Early in 1850, Dickens founded the first of the weekly magazines that were to continue publication until his death. *Household Words* heralded his career as editor and joint owner of a magazine, receiving a salary and a share in the profits of the venture. In his preliminary words, an early indication of the subject-matter of *Hard Times*, he made clear that the purpose of the publication was to 'cherish that light of Fancy which is inherent in the human breast. Its many crusades included proper sewage disposal, cheap and unlimited supply of water, the replacement of slums by decent housing for the poor, the establishment of playgrounds for children and government aid for public education. David Trotter's comments in his introduction to the Penguin edition of *Great Expectations* are particularly appropriate in this context:

> It would not reduce Dickens's politics absurdly to say that he was for circulation and against stoppage, and that he wasn't at all afraid of the literal application of the metaphor to everyday existence. He thought that the lives of the poor could only be made tolerable by the proper circulation of air and water through their living quarters. He was sickened by physical blockage, by enclosed congested spaces in the centre of the city, like Smithfield Market, or urban burial grounds (1117 corpses per acre, according to *Household Words*, giving off 55.261 cubic feet of noxious gases per acre per year).
>
> (p. xv)

The extension of free trading and the promotion of commercial interchange were advocated in *Household Words* and they act as a backdrop for Pip's altruistic concern in *Great Expectations* for the promotion of Herbert Pocket's financial enterprises as he tries to force a distinction between clean and dirty money.

In November 1851 Dickens began *Bleak House*, the last of the novels which he wrote as part of the 1844 agreement with Bradbury and Evans and it was begun during the arrangements he made to move home to Tavistock House. In a letter to the Hon. Mrs Richard Watson, November 1852, Dickens noted that its immediate success was to make its circulation 'half as large again as Copperfield' (Johnson, vol. 2, p. 756). Appearing in monthly parts between March 1852 and September 1853, *Bleak House* takes as its context the self-satisfaction of an England which had witnessed the Great Exhibition of 1851. The *Manchester Guardian* had referred to that year as one in which there were 'good grounds for satisfaction, for hope, and for self-approval' but Dickens's novel highlights the internal rottenness of the social structure, the fog which suffocates creative energy and the crumbling of Tom-all-Alone's which works its retribution through all levels of the social scene. Dickens took its name from a Chatham memory of a house erected by a recluse behind Fort Pitt fields and its description in the novel has echoes of the blacking factory stain:

> Now, these tumbling tenements contain, by night, a swarm of misery. As, on the ruined human wretch, vermin parasites appear, so these ruined shelters have bred a crowd of foul existence that crawls in and out of gaps in walls and boards . . .
>
> (*Bleak House*, p. 220)

After a European tour in December 1853 Dickens gave the first public readings of his books at the Birmingham Town Hall, in aid of the Literary and Scientific Institute. Recognizing that the profits made by *Household Words* had slipped badly over the past six months Dickens decided to produce a new novel in weekly parts. In a letter to Mrs Watson he suggested that the new idea had 'laid hold of me by the throat in a very violent manner' (Johnson, vol. 2, p. 793), and the abstract defences put up by economists to clear the consciences of the materialistically greedy became *Hard times*. Written in less than six months, this novel records Dickens's violent hostility to the inhumane growth of industrial capitalism and the prison-like enclosure of a factory world.

This sense of helpless imprisonment became the central motif of *Little Dorrit* which was published in monthly parts between December 1855 and June 1857. The pervading image of the prison which haunts *Little Dorrit* has its root in the growing unhappiness of Dickens's marriage to Catherine, as well as his frustration at seeing the restraint which social forces were putting upon human vitality. The former unhappiness had been given an eerie perspective when he was contacted by Maria Beadnell (now Winter) only to discover that his former 'love' had become, in her words, 'toothless, fat, old and ugly' (Johnson, vol. 2, p. 833). The effect of social machinery was to produce a society which was, in Edgar Johnson's words, 'a vast jail . . . in which the people and their governors were captives and wardens dwelling within the same confining walls' (*ibid.*, p. 883).

In May 1858 Charles and Catherine Dickens separated amid acrimonious accusations and an announcement in *Household Words* that 'all the lately whispered rumours' are groundless. Although there was no new novel being worked on at this time, Dickens had started the public readings of which he was to continue for the rest of his life. The personal announcement in *Household Words* prompted a major disagreement with the publishers, Bradbury and Evans, and led to the magazine's closure in March 1859 and the immediate opening of a new weekly, *All the Year Round*. Getting this new magazine off successfully, Dickens began the serialization of *A Tale of Two Cities* much of which he wrote at his new house, the long-coveted Gad's Hill Place. His London home was put up for sale and Dickens seemed determined to make a decisive break with the past by burning his accumulation of letters and papers from the past 20 years. The success of *All the Year Round* was immediate and was kept going by the serialization of Wilkie Collins's *The Woman in White*. However, to follow Collins's novel Dickens chose a work by Charles Lever and the serialization of *A Day's Ride* led to a dramatic falling off of sales. Although he had only been contributing a series of autobiographical personal essays under the title *The Uncommercial Traveller* since the completion of *A Tale of Two Cities* in October 1859, he now decided to boost flagging sales by starting a new novel, *Great Expectations*. In a letter to the Earl of Carlisle, August 1860, Dickens refers to 'prowling about, meditating a new book' (*Letters of Charles Dickens: Volume 9*, p. 284) and at this stage it had been conceived as a serial story in the form of 20 monthly parts. By October 1860, Dickens was writing to Forster that he felt the need to boost flagging sales of *All the Year Round* by writing the new book in 36 weekly instalments: 'I must make the most I can out of the book. You shall have the first two or three weekly parts to-morrow. The name is GREAT EXPECTATIONS. I think a good name?' (Forster, p. 567). In an earlier letter to Forster he had mentioned that 'a very fine, new, and grotesque idea has opened upon me . . . it so opens out before *me* that I can see the whole of a serial revolving on it, in a most singular and comic manner' (*ibid.*, p. 516) Referring to the walks Dickens took around his Gad's Hill home, Forster points to the opening chapter of the new novel:

To another drearier churchyard, itself forming part of the marshes beyond the Medway, he often took friends to show them

the dozen small tombstones of various sizes adapted to the
respective ages of a dozen small children of one family . . . About
the whole of this Cooling churchyard, indeed, and the neighbour-
ing castle ruins, there was a weird strangeness that made it one of
his attractive walks in the late year or winter . . .

(*ibid.*, p. 516)

As Janice Carlisle points out in her introduction to the Bedford
edition of *Great Expectations*, the decision to publish the new story
in weekly parts 'largely accounts for the unity and concision' of the
novel and the autobiographical narrative style has an immediate
dramatic impact (p. 17). Four of the first six novels published in the
magazine used this formula.

Highly successful public readings of his work occupied Dickens
for the next four years, and as Edgar Johnson reports, 'Gold now
poured itself out for Dickens in an endless stream. Advance sheets
of his novels brought him handsome sums from Harper and
Brothers in New York. Whenever he wished he could obtain £1,000
for a short story. The sales of *All the Year Round*, already risen with
the publication of *Great Expectations* to several thousands higher
than the *London Times*, continued rising and *Great Expectations*
went into a fourth edition within a few weeks of its appearance in
book form' (Johnson, vol. 2, p. 995).

By the end of 1863 Dickens was anxious to begin a new novel, *Our
Mutual Friend*, which was published by Chapman and Hall in 20
monthly parts. This dark and bitter last novel takes place in the
mazes of London and centres around the dust-heaps off which a
scavenging society feeds.

The last years of his life were dominated by the exhausting and
highly successful public readings which took a devastating toll upon
his health, and Charles Dickens died from a brain haemorrhage in
June 1870, leaving his last novel, *Edwin Drood*, unfinished.

Dates	Biography	Literary context	Historical context
1812	CD born in Portsmouth	Byron's *Childe Harold*, cantos i and ii	Napoleon invades Russia
1813	Dickens family move to Southsea	Austen's *Pride and Prejudice*	
1817	Move to Chatham	Coleridge's *Biographia Literaria*; Keats's *Poems*	
1821	CD starts at William Giles's school	De Quincey's *Confessions of an English Opium Eater*	Greek War of Independence
1822	Move to London; CD breaks off schooling	Byron's *Vision of Judgement*	
1824	CD starts at Warren's Blacking Factory; John Dickens imprisoned in Marshalsea	Landor's *Imaginary Conversations*	Repeal of Combination Acts
1825	CD starts at Wellington House Academy	Hazlitt's *Spirit of the Age*	Stockton–Darlington railway opened
1827	CD becomes solicitor's clerk	Constable's 'Cornfield'	Battle of Navarino
1829	CD becomes reporter at Doctors' Commons	Turner's 'Ulysses Deriding Polyphemus'	Catholic Emancipation Act; Peel's Metropolitan Police in London founded
1830	CD meets Maria Beadnell	Tennyson's *Poems, Chiefly Lyrical*	Revolution in France
1831	CD becomes reporter for *The Mirror of Parliament*	Hugo's *Notre Dame de Paris*	
1832	CD becomes reporter for *True Sun*	Lytton's *Eugene Aram*	Reform Bill passed
1834	CD becomes reporter on *The Morning Chronicle*; meets Catherine Hogarth	Ainsworth's *Rookwood*; Lytton's *Last Days of Pompeii*	Poor Law Amendment Act; Transportation of Tolpuddle Martyrs; burning of Houses of Parliament
1836	Marries Catherine Hogarth; meets John Forster	**Sketches by Boz** (First Series); **Pickwick Papers** begins;	
1837	First child born; death of Mary Hogarth; first visit to Europe	**Oliver Twist** begins; Carlyle's *French Revolution*	Accession of Victoria
1838	Second child born	**Nicholas Nickleby** begins	Anti-Corn Law League founded

Dates	Biography	Literary context	Historical context
1839	Third child born	Ainsworth's *Jack Sheppard*	
1840		***Master Humphrey's Clock: The Old Curiosity Shop*** begins	Marriage of Victoria and Albert
1841	Fourth child born	***Barnaby Rudge***	Peel becomes Prime Minister
1842	CD visits America	***American Notes***; ***Martin Chuzzlewit*** begins	
1843		***A Christmas Carol***; Carlyle's *Past and Present*	Rotherhithe Tunnel built
1844	Fifth child born; moves to Genoa	***The Chimes***; Disraeli's *Coningsby*	
1845	Sixth child born; visits Rome, Naples	***The Cricket on the Hearth***; Disraeli's *Sybil*	
1846	CD becomes editor of *The Daily News*; moves to Lausanne, Paris	***Pictures from Italy***; ***Dombey and Son*** begins; ***The Battle of Life***	Irish famine; repeal of Corn Laws
1847	Seventh child born	Emily Brontë's *Wuthering Heights*	Factory Act
1848	Directs and acts in plays for the Amateur Players	***The Haunted Man***; Mrs Gaskell's *Mary Barton*	European revolutions
1849	Eighth child born	***David Copperfield*** begins; Charlotte Brontë's *Shirley*	
1850	Ninth child born; founds Guild of Literature and Art	Start of ***Household Words***; Tennyson's *In Memoriam*	
1851	Amateur theatricals at Rockingham Castle; CD moves to Tavistock House	***Child's History of England***; Ruskin's *Stones of Venice*	The Great Exhibition
1852	Tenth child born	***Bleak House*** begins; Thackeray's *Henry Esmond*	
1853	First Public Reading in Birmingham	Charlotte Brontë's *Villette*;	
1854		***Hard Times***	Outbreak of Crimean War

CONTEXTS

Dates	Biography	Literary context	Historical context
1855	CD directs and acts in Wilkie Collins's *The Lighthouse*	*Little Dorrit* begins; Trollope's *The Warden*	Fall of Sebastopol
1856	CD buys Gad's Hill Place	Flaubert's *Madame Bovary*	End of Crimean War
1857	CD directs and acts in Collins's *The Frozen Deep*; meets Ellen Ternan	*The Lazy Tour of Two Idle Apprentices*; Baudelaire's *Les Fleurs du Mal*	Indian Mutiny
1858	CD separates from Catherine; first provincial Reading Tour	George Eliot's *Scenes from Clerical Life*	Abolition of East India Company
1859	Second provincial Reading Tour	*A Tale of Two Cities* begins in *All The Year Round*; George Eliot's *Adam Bede*	
1860	CD settles permanently in Gad's Hill	*The Uncommercial Traveller*; first instalment of *Great Expectations*; Collins's *The Woman in White*; Eliot's *The Mill on the Floss*	
1861	Third provincial Reading Tour	*Great Expectations* published in two volumes; Eliot's *Silas Marner*	Outbreak of American Civil War
1862		Hugo's *Les Miserables*; Ruskin's *Unto This Last*	Bismark becomes Prime Minister of Prussia
1863	CD conducts charity readings at British Embassy, Paris	Kingsley's *The Water Babies*	Work begins on the London Underground Railway
1864		*Our Mutual Friend* begins	First Trades Union Conference
1865	CD and Ellen Ternan in Staplehurst railway disaster	Lewis Carroll's *Alice in Wonderland*	
1866	CD reading tour in London and the provinces	Eliot's *Felix Holt*	Opening of Dr Barnado's home for destitute children in East London
1867	CD reading tour in England, Ireland and America	*No Thoroughfare*; Zola's *Thérèse Raquin*	

Dates	Biography	Literary context	Historical context
1868	CD leaves New York for England	Collin's *The Moonstone*	
1869	First public reading of 'Sikes and Nancy'; reading tour broken off on account of illness	Arnold's *Culture and Anarchy*	
1870	Last readings; CD dies of a brain haemorrhage at Gad's Hill	***Edwin Drood*** begins and is left unfinished	Franco–Prussian War; First Elementary Education Act for England and Wales

STUDY QUESTIONS

1. The early life of Charles Dickens in Chatham and Rochester seems to have held a magnetic importance for the novelist throughout his life. How can you relate these early biographical details to your reading of *Great Expectations*?

2. The shadow of the prison-house seems to hang over much of Dickens's early life. How can you draw together themes from the novelist's biography and the doom-laden sense of loss which haunts *Great Expectations*?

3. The nineteenth century was a period of enormous change with unavoidable impacts upon both the physical and the psychological context of growing up. In what ways do the industrial changes and the urban growth of this period inform the mood and tone of *Great Expectations*?

CHAPTER 2

LANGUAGE, FORM AND STYLE

In his analysis of *Little Dorrit*, Edgar Johnson refers to Dickens's lifelong preoccupation with prisons:

> From the early Visit to Newgate in *Sketches by Boz*, through Mr. Pickwick's detention in the Fleet, the frightful description of Fagin in the condemned cell, and Mr. Micawber's incarceration in the King's Bench, to the unwritten ending of *The Mystery of Edwin Drood*, in which the murderer was to gasp out his confession in another prison cell, the sombre theme runs like a dark thread through all Dickens's work.
>
> (Johnson, vol. 2, p. 884)

Johnson recognizes the compulsion that led Dickens to return to the pervading image of the Marshalsea prison which dominates *Little Dorrit* as revealing the depth of the wound caused by his childhood humiliation and grief:

> It shows that he still felt a need to explore the meaning of that painful area in his own past on a deeper level than he had been able to plumb in *David Copperfield*. And it bears witness to how profoundly the prison had sunk into his consciousness as a symbol of misery and defeat.
>
> (Johnson, vol. 2, p. 885)

In the autobiographical writing from which Forster quotes so extensively, the all-pervasive nature of the stain of imprisonment and guilt, associated with being cast off by his parents to work in the Blacking Warehouse, was recorded in haunting terms:

> My whole nature was so penetrated with the grief and humiliation of such considerations that, even now – famous and caressed and happy – I often forget in my dreams that I have a dear wife and children – even that I am a man – and wander desolately back to that time of my life.
>
> (*ibid.*, pp. 26–7)

That haunting presence of the Hungerford Stairs experience was such that

> Until old Hungerford Market was pulled down, until old Hungerford Stairs were destroyed, and the very nature of the ground changed, I never had the courage to go back to the place where my servitude began. I never saw it. I could not endure to go near it. For many years, when I came near to Robert Warren's in the Strand, I crossed over to the opposite side of the way to avoid a certain smell of the cement they put upon the blacking-corks, which reminded me of what I was once.
>
> (*ibid.*, pp. 26–7)

However, the inescapable power of those early experiences resurfaces regardless of any avoidance tactics taken, in a manner that Pip was later to discover when confronted by Trabb's boy in chapter 30 of *Great Expectations*. Having arrived at the Blue Boar, in his home town, and feeling that his 'position was a distinguished one', Pip is seen by 'that unlimited miscreant, Trabb's boy' and is ludicrously highlighted by the comic antics of mock-respect which finally leave him fleeing the town:

> The disgrace attendant on his immediately afterwards taking to crowing and pursuing me across the bridge with crows, as from an exceedingly dejected fowl who had known me when I was a blacksmith, culminated the disgrace with which I left the town, and was, so to speak, ejected by it into the open country.

Pip's morbid sense of shame at his background is also highlighted when Joe pays him a visit in London, chapter 27, and tells him that 'me and Wopsle went off straight to look at the Blacking Ware'us'. The 'taint in the arrangement' of leaving home accompanied by Joe at the end of the first 'Stage' is kept alive throughout the embarrassment of this visit to Barnard's Inn.

In the earlier prison novel, *Little Dorrit*, when William Dorrit is released from the Marshalsea after 23 years of incarceration he travels abroad with his daughter, Amy, who had been born within the walls of the prison. However, the taint of those years of imprisonment cannot be washed clean by newly acquired wealth and the social standing which wealth supposedly brings; Amy, like her father, can never shake herself free from the past:

> Sitting opposite her father in the travelling-carriage, and recalling the old Marshalsea room, her present existence was a dream. All that she saw was new and wonderful, but it was not real; it seemed to her as if those visions of mountains and picturesque countries might melt away at any moment, and the carriage, turning some abrupt corner, bring up with a jolt at the old Marshalsea gate.
>
> (*Little Dorrit* Book 2, chapter 3)

As the Dorrit family stay at the convent of the Great Saint Bernard on the route down to Italy, the old 'Father of the Marshalsea', who desperately hopes to conceal his past beneath a veneer of money, cannot help referring to what he sees as 'the confinement' of the convent, 'the space . . . So small. So – ha – very limited'. He urges this view on his host, the Abbot, that 'the space was so – ha – hum – so very contracted. More than that. It was always the same, always the same.'

When summoned down to Kent by Miss Havisham, in chapter 28 of *Great Expectations*, Pip, accompanied by Herbert, catches the afternoon coach from Cross Keys and has an unnerving meeting with the past that he assumed had disappeared for ever, as two convicts are 'going down with me':

> One was a taller and stouter man than the other, and appeared as a matter of course, according to the mysterious ways of the world both convict and free, to have had allotted to him the smaller suit of clothes. His arms and legs were like great pin-cushions of those

shapes, and his attire disguised him absurdly; but I knew his half-closed eye at one glance. There stood the man whom I had seen on the settle at the Three Jolly Bargemen on a Saturday night, and who had brought me down with his invisible gun!

The Marshalsea Prison which housed John Dickens and his family for three months in 1824 was closed in 1842, when an Act of Parliament reduced the incidence of imprisonment for debt. The buildings were sold and used by an ironmonger, but Dickens revisited the area surrounding Borough High Street in 1855. As he informed Forster: 'Went to the Borough yesterday morning before going to Gadshill, to see if I could find any ruins of the Marshalsea. Found a great part of the original building – now "Marshalsea Place." Found the rooms that have been in my mind's eye in the story' (*Letters: Volume 8*, p. 321).

The world of the 'little-boy-lost' is central to Dickens's novels throughout his career and it is worth noting how commonplace it is for him to concentrate on disabled family-life in relation to the rearing of children. The list of isolated children include Oliver Twist (orphan), Little Nell (no father or mother), Barnaby Rudge (abandoned by his father who is a murderer), Nicholas Nickleby (no father), Florence Dombey (no mother; indifferent father), David Copperfield (no father; early loss of mother; brutal step-father), Esther Summerson (orphan), Arthur Clennam (no father; severe and imprisoning mother), Pip (orphan; adopted by a convict). In his New Year's article of 1 January 1853, written for *Household Words* and entitled 'Where We Stopped Growing', Dickens highlights his firm belief that the preservation of a child's sense of wonder is central to the healthy development into adulthood. He draws attention to the importance for him of reading *Robinson Crusoe*, *The Arabian Nights* and *Don Quixote*, before telling us that

We have never outgrown the rugged walls of Newgate, or any other prison on the outside. All within, is still the same blank of remorse and misery . . . We have never outgrown the wicked old Bastille. Here, in our mind at this present childish moment, is a distinct groundplan (wholly imaginative and resting on no sort of authority), of a maze of low vaulted passages with small black doors; and here, inside of this remote door on the left, where the black cobwebs hang like a veil from the arch, and the jailer's lamp will scarcely burn, was shut up, in black silence through so many years, that old man of the affecting anecdote, who was at last set free. But, who brought his white face, and his white hair, and his phantom figure, back again, to tell them what they had made him – how he had no wife, no child, no friend, no recognition of the light and air – and prayed to be shut up in his old dungeon till he died.

(*Dickens' Journalism', vol. 3*)

The prison as a building, as architecture, is central to Georges Bataille's argument, quoted in Denis Hollier's *Against Architecture: The Writings of Georges Bataille* (1989):

Architecture is the expression of the very soul of societies, just as human physiognomy is the expression of the individuals' souls. It is, however, particularly to the physiognomies of official personages . . . that this comparison pertains . . . Great monuments are erected like dikes, opposing the logic and majesty of authority against all disturbing elements . . . monuments inspire social prudence and often real fear. The taking of the Bastille is symbolic of this state of things: it is hard to explain this crowd movement other than by the animosity of the people against the monuments that are their real masters.

However, as Dickens recognized throughout his novels, the stain of imprisonment exists far beyond the destruction of brick and stone. In his memories of the prison in Philadelphia, recorded in *American Notes*, he observed:

On the haggard face of every man among these prisoners, the same expression sat. I know not what to like it to. It had something of that strained attention which we see upon the faces of the blind and deaf, mingled with a kind of horror, as though they had all been secretly terrified. In every little chamber that I entered, and at every grate through which I looked, I seemed to see the same appalling countenance. It lives in my memory, with the fascination of a remarkable picture . . .

My firm conviction is that, independent of the mental anguish it occasions – an anguish so acute and so tremendous, that all imagination of it must fall far short of the reality – it wears the mind into a morbid state, which renders it unfit for the rough contact and busy action of the world. It is my fixed opinion that those who have undergone this punishment, MUST pass into society again morally unhealthy and diseased.

(pp. 108–9)

In *A Tale of Two Cities*, Dr Manette exists in a garret room after his release from prison and Monsieur Defarge keeps the door locked 'Because he has lived so long, locked up, that he would be frightened – rave – tear himself to pieces – die – come to I know not what harm – if his door was left open' (p. 35).

The Eastern Penitentiary at Philadelphia was founded in 1830 on the principles of Jeremy Bentham's Panopticon and its example was followed in London by the creation of Pentonville Prison in 1842. The architectural design and moral and educational purposes of Bentham's Panopticon, or Inspection House, is described by Michel Foucault in his *Discipline and Punish: The Birth of the Prison*:

. . . at the periphery, an annular building; at the centre, a tower; this tower is pierced with wide windows that open onto the inner side of the ring; the peripheric building is divided into cells, each of which extends the whole width of the building; they have two windows, one on the inside, corresponding to the windows of the tower; the other, on the outside, allows the light to cross the cell from one end to the other. All that is needed, then, is to place a supervisor in a central tower and to shut up in each cell a madman, a patient, a condemned man, a worker or a schoolboy. By the effect of backlighting, one can observe from the tower, standing out precisely against the light, the small captive shadows in the cells of the periphery. They are like so many cages, so many small theatres, in which each actor is alone, perfectly individualized and constantly visible. The panoptic mechanism arranges spatial unities that make it possible to see constantly and to recognize immediately. In short, it reverses the principle of the dungeon; or rather of its three functions – to enclose, to deprive of light and to hide – it preserves only the first and eliminates the other two. Full lighting and the eye of a supervisor capture better than darkness, which ultimately protected. Visibility is a trap.

(p. 200)

The Panopticon as a mechanism of power acts directly on individuals, giving power of mind over mind, and in his prefatory statement concerning its uses, Bentham eulogizes on 'a great and new instrument of government . . .; its great excellence consists in the great strength it is capable of giving to **any** institution it may be thought proper to apply it to' (quoted in Foucault, p. 206). With the passing of the 1779 Penitentiary Act there was an implicit shift of meaning within the prison world where simple incarceration was replaced by a purposeful move to produce guilt and repentance.

According to the autobiographical writing quoted by Forster, when Dickens began work at the blacking warehouse 'There was a recess in it, in which I was to sit and work', and his employer 'had kindly arranged to teach me something in the dinner-hour' (Forster, p. 18). This arrangement, however, soon became overlooked, and 'my small work-table and my grosses of pots, papers, string, scissors, paste-pot, and labels, by little and little, vanished out of the recess in the counting-house, and kept company with the other small work-tables, grosses of pots, papers, string, scissors, and paste-pots downstairs' (*ibid.*). Some time after the release of John Dickens from the Marshalsea, the blacking business moved to Covent Garden and was more immediately visible to all passers-by:

> We worked, for the light's sake, near the second window as you come from Bedford Street; and we were so brisk at it, that the people used to stop and look in. Sometimes there would be quite a little crowd there. I saw my father coming in the door one day when we were very busy, and I wondered how he could bear it.
>
> (*ibid.*, p. 26)

This morbid awareness of being overlooked and its association with both threat and guilt is startlingly vivid in chapter 34 of *Oliver Twist*, where the boy 'sat at this window intent upon his books'. He is in Mr Brownlow's house, and is therefore ostensibly secure while he dozes in 'the first shades of twilight':

> There is a kind of sleep that steals upon us sometimes, which, while it holds the body prisoner, does not free the mind from a sense of things about it, and enable it to ramble at its pleasure . . .

Oliver knew, perfectly well, that he was in his own little room; that his books were lying on the table before him; that the sweet air was stirring among the creeping plants outside. And yet he was asleep. Suddenly, the scene changed; the air became close and confined; and he thought, with a glow of terror, that he was in the Jew's house again. There sat the hideous old man, in his accustomed corner, pointing at him, and whispering to another man, with his face averted, who sat beside him.

The illustration by George Cruikshank which accompanies this scene conveys the nightmarish sense of being watched and this dream-like sequence is a prelude to what happens to William Dorrit as the past comes storming in on him at a social reception in *Little Dorrit*, Book 2, chapter 19. Having tried to varnish over the past 23 years of imprisonment and its social stain, William Dorrit stands up at a Roman banquet to announce:

Ladies and gentlemen, the duty – ha – devolves upon me of – hum – welcoming you to the Marshalsea. Welcome to the Marshalsea! The space is – ha – limited – limited – the parade might be wider; but you will find it apparently grow larger after a time – a time, ladies and gentlemen – and the air is, all things considered, very good.

The architectural and optical system of surveillance can be used to reform prisoners but also to treat patients, to confine the insane, to supervise workers in a factory or to instruct schoolchildren. In terms of the first of these, the notes which Dickens made concerning the Eastern Penitentiary herald the chapter towards the end of *David Copperfield*, where we are shown 'Two Interesting Penitents'. The system of solitary confinement in Philadelphia raised in Dickens a considerable degree of scepticism:

Standing at the central point, and looking down these dreary passages, the dull repose and quiet that prevails, is awful. Occasionally, there is a drowsy sound from some lone weaver's shuttle, or shoemaker's last, but it is stifled by the thick walls and heavy dungeon-door, and only serves to make the general stillness more profound.

Dickens commented on the prisoners being 'buried alive'; they are reduced to being a number placed over the cell door which finds an echo in the 'plain, bare, monotonous vault of a schoolroom' opening the first chapter of *Hard Times*. In the 'Facts' system of education preached by Mr Gradgrind, and put into practice by Mr M'Choakumchild, the boys and girls 'sat on the face of the inclined plane in two compact bodies, divided up the centre by a narrow interval'. The teacher's eye is able to roam freely over the numbered pupils before firing his cannons of questions at them which will 'blow them clean out of the regions of childhood at one discharge.' Similar to the description of the Eastern Penitentiary where 'the perfect order of the building cannot be praised too highly', and the 'excellent motives of all who are immediately concerned in the administration of the system' cannot be doubted, Gradgrind seems 'a galvanising apparatus, too, charged with a grim mechanical substitute for the tender young imaginations that were to be stormed away.' The organized mechanistic observation of those 'penitents' who need to acknowledge their sin and their worthlessness linguistically spills over into the way in which Wemmick refers to Jaggers in *Great Expectations*, chapter 24:

> Wemmick was at his desk, lunching – and crunching – on a dry hard biscuit; pieces of which he threw from time to time into his slit of a mouth, as if he were posting them.
>
> 'Always seems to me,' said Wemmick, 'as if he had set a man-trap and was watching it. Suddenly – click – you're caught!'

The architectural design of observation and power traps the 'Hands' in the mills of Coketown in chapter 11 of *Hard Times*:

> So many hundred of Hands in this Mill; so many hundred horse Steam Power. It is known, to the force of a single pound weight, what the engine will do; but, not all the calculators of the National Debt can tell me the capacity for good or evil, for love or hatred, for patriotism or discontent, for the decomposition of virtue into vice, or the reverse, at any single moment in the soul of one of these its quiet servants, with the composed faces and the regulated actions.

Foucault recognizes that the Panopticon provided a 'type of location of bodies in space, of distribution of individuals in relation to one another, of hierarchical organisation, of disposition of centres and channels of power, which can be implemented in hospital, workshops, schools, prisons' (p. 205). In the development of that little seed, Pip, the controllers within the prison system watch him carefully. He has already been informed at Christmas dinner, in chapter 4, that the young are always 'Naterally wicious' and the guests around the table 'looked at me in a particularly unpleasant and personal manner'. Later on, when Pip requests time off work to go and visit Miss Havisham in chapter 15, we are told that 'My sister had been standing silent in the yard, within hearing – she was a most unscrupulous spy and listener – and she instantly looked in at one of the windows.' Her interference leads to the fight between Orlick and Joe, and is a link in that chain of events which leads to her being struck down with the piece of convict's chain. Pip feels a sense of guilt from within the cell of his own mind, and that guilt may well be related to an unacknowledged feeling that Orlick has only done what he, Pip, wanted to achieve. As a controller, Mrs Joe watches the fight between her husband and Orlick before being carried into the house in a similar way to that in which Estella watches Pip's fight with 'the pale young gentleman', and Miss Havisham watches Estella 'beggar' Pip at cards.

This feeling of being the object of observation and its connections with guilt and shame are central to the story 'George Silverman's Explanation', published in *All the Year Round*, February 1868. Written in the first person, like *Great Expectations*, George describes his 'infant home' as a cellar in Preston. Surrounded by abject poverty he describes his mother descending the steps to the cellar in a way that might recall the arrival of a gaoler:

> I recollect the sound of father's Lancashire clogs on the street pavement above, as being different in my young hearing from the sound of all other clogs; and I recollect, that, when mother came down the cellar-steps, I used tremblingly to speculate on her feet having a good or an ill-tempered look, – on her knees, – on her waist, – until finally her face came into view, and settled the question. From this it will be seen that I was timid, and that the cellar-steps were steep, and that the doorway was very low.
>
> (*The Uncommercial Traveller and Reprinted Pieces*, p. 730)

As a parallel to Pip's being reminded of his natural viciousness and his likelihood of ending up on the gallows for asking questions, George has it drilled into him that he is a 'worldly little devil':

> And the sting of it was, that I quite well knew myself to be a worldly little devil. Worldly as to be wanting to be housed and warmed, worldly as to wanting to be fed, worldly as to the greed with which I inwardly compared how much I got of those good things with how much father and mother got, when rarely, those good things were going.
>
> Sometimes they both went away seeking work; and then I would be locked up in the cellar for a day or two at a time. I was at my worldliest then. Left alone, I yielded myself up to a worldly yearning for enough of anything (except misery), and for the death of mother's father, who was a machine-maker at Birmingham, and on whose decease, I had heard mother say, she would come into a whole courtful of houses 'if she had her rights'. Worldly little devil, I would stand about, musingly fitting my cold bare feet into cracked bricks and crevices of the damp cellar-floor, – walking over my grandfather's body, so to speak, into the courtful of houses, and selling them for meat and drink, and clothes to wear.
>
> (*ibid.*)

There are echoes here of the history Magwitch gives of himself in chapter 42 of *Great Expectations*, where he refers to himself as 'a ragged little creetur' who soon 'got the name of being hardened':

> 'This is a terrible hardened one,' they says to prison wisitors, picking out me. 'May be said to live in jails, this boy.' Then they looked at me, and I looked at them, and they measured my head, some on 'em – they had better a measured my stomach – and others on 'em give me tracts what I couldn't read, and made me speeches what I couldn't understand.

As if the controller of the Panopticon has read his mind, when George is rescued from the cellar after both parents have died, he finds himself the object of some interest:

> The ring of people widened outward from the inner side as I looked around me; and I smelt vinegar, and what I know to be

camphor, thrown in towards where I sat. Presently some one put a great vessel of smoking vinegar on the ground near me; and then they all looked at me in silent horror as I ate and drank of what was brought for me. I knew at the time they had a horror of me, but I couldn't help it.

(The Uncommercial Traveller, p. 732)

Dickens's preoccupation with imprisonment and its attendant sense of guilt and shame is central to his early 'A Visit to Newgate', published in *Sketches by Boz* (pp. 201–14). Here, the sense of 'wretched creatures' being 'pent up' makes Newgate 'this gloomy depository of the guilt and misery of London'. As people pass by the prison they are unknowing or unheeding of the fact that 'as they pass one particular angle of the massive wall with a light laugh or a merry whistle, they stand within one yard of a fellow-creature, bound and helpless, whose hours are numbered, from whom the last feeble ray of hope has fled for ever, and whose miserable career will shortly terminate in a violent and shameful death.' As the author arrives for his journalistic inspection he enters a small room which has a shelf 'on which were a few boxes of papers, and casts of the heads and faces of the two notorious murderers, Bishop and Williams'. Like their counterparts on the shelf in Jaggers's office, they have an unpleasant appearance and the one of Bishop 'might have afforded sufficient moral grounds for his instant execution at any time, even had there been no other evidence against him.' Unlike the model penitentiaries of the next decade, the Newgate of the 1830s which we are presented with is a maze of 'tortuous and intricate windings' which are guarded by 'huge gates and gratings'. However, the solitary system is anticipated here by the enclosed manner in which the prisoners take little notice of each other and 'who were no more concerned by what was passing before their eyes, and within their hearing, than if they were blind and deaf'. Unlike the sensitive young Dickens in the blacking warehouse, the frightened Pip of *Great Expectations* or the self-doubting George Silverman, the 14 young boys who are lined up for the inspection visit show no shame or contrition: 'There was not one redeeming feature among them – not a glance of honesty – not a wink expressive of anything but the gallows and the hulks, in the whole collection.' With all 14 being committed for trial on charges of 'pocket-picking' they stand like a troop of Fagin's boys in *Oliver Twist*. The description of the condemned cell in this sketch also acts as a type of first draft of the harrowing visit which Oliver makes to Fagin on the eve of his execution. The only escape which is open to the condemned man is the world of dream when, 'worn with watching and excitement' he falls asleep to find himself 'walking with his wife in a pleasant field, with the bright sky above them, and a fresh and boundless prospect on every side – how different from the stone walls of Newgate.' As the dream alters its scene, he finds himself on trial again:

> . . . there are the judge and jury, and prosecutors, and witnesses, just as they were before. How full the court is – what a sea of heads – with a gallows, too, and a scaffold – and how all those people stare at *him!* Verdict, 'Guilty.' No matter; he will escape.

When the Newgate sketch was published, a paragraph in the *Morning Chronicle*, praising its publication, likened it to Victor Hugo's *Dernier Jour d'un Condamné* where the spectacle of an execution leads to an unhealthy sense of voyeurism. In his 1832 Preface, Hugo, referring to himself in the third person, tells the reader that he found the inspiration for his work 'lying in a pool of blood under the red stumps of the guillotine' and in imagery which anticipates Wemmick walking 'among the prisoners, much as a gardener might walk among his plants' in his 'greenhouse' (*Great Expectations*, chapter 32), he suggests that 'the scaffold is the only construction that revolutions do not demolish':

> For rarely are revolutions innocent of human blood and, since they occur in order to dock, lop, and pollard society, the death penalty is one of the pruning blades they surrender most unwillingly.
>
> (Hugo, p. 5)

Hugo also emphasizes the prisoner's sense of being the constant focus of attention. When he is alone in his individual cell, 'there is a man on guard in front of my cell door, so that my glance never strays to the square peep-hole without meeting his two wide, staring eyes.' When he is taken into court,

> As I came into view, there was a rustle of arms and voices, the noise of seats being moved and partitions creaking. While I walked the

whole length of the room, between two crowds of spectators held back by soldiers, I felt like the nodal point to which were connected the nerves that operated all those vacant faces and craning necks.

(*ibid.*, p. 27)

The fantasy which allows the prisoner to seem to escape from his confinement is sketched out in chapter 7 of *American Notes*, where we are told that there was a German sentenced to five years' imprisonment for larceny who had painted 'every inch of the walls and ceiling quite beautifully'. Dickens comments upon 'the taste and ingenuity' of this man, although it seems to have little effect since he is a 'heart-broken, wretched creature'. In a similar manner, as a way of escaping from the debts, shortage of paid labour and confinement of Bleeding Heart Yard in *Little Dorrit*, Mrs Plornish's parlour is decorated with an ingenious fiction which consists of the wall 'being painted to represent the exterior of a thatched cottage':

The modest sun-flower and holly-hock were depicted as flourishing with great luxuriance on this rustic dwelling, while a quantity of dense smoke issuing from the chimney indicated good cheer within, and, also, perhaps, that it had not been lately swept. A faithful dog was represented as flying at the legs of the friendly visitor, from the threshold; and a circular pigeon-house, enveloped in a cloud of pigeons, arose from behind the garden-paling.

(*Little Dorrit* Book 2, chapter 13)

The replacement of one version of reality by another, the fiction created to make the sordid confinement more bearable, is perhaps felt most perversely in *Little Dorrit* in the manner in which the 'Father of the Marshalsea' pities those who are unable to share the security and comfort of imprisonment. The doctor, an inmate who assisted at the prison-birth of Amy, tells William Dorrit that 'A little more elbow-room is all we want here':

We are quiet here; we don't get badgered here; there's no knocker here, sir, to be hammered at by creditors and bring a man's heart into his mouth. Nobody comes here to ask if a man's at home, and to say he'll stand on the door mat till he is. Nobody writes threatening letters about money, to this place. It's freedom, sir, it's freedom!

An interesting connection might be seen here when Wemmick first takes Pip home to his 'castle' in Walworth in chapter 25 of *Great Expecations*: 'It appeared to be a collection of back lanes, ditches, and little gardens' and the house 'was a little wooden cottage in the midst of plots of garden, and the top of it was cut out and painted like a battery mounted with guns.' The need for Wemmick to keep his private identity separate from his official one at 'Little Britain' is further emphasized by the fiction of crossing a drawbridge which is withdrawn as soon as the visitors are safely within the 'castle' grounds:

> The bridge was a plank, and it crossed a chasm about four feet wide and two deep. But it was very pleasant to see the pride with which he hoisted it up and made it fast; smiling as he did so, with a relish and not merely mechanically.

Having crossed the moat, there is still some ingenious difficulty in getting to the house as 'he conducted me to a bower about a dozen yards off . . . approached by such ingenious twists of path that it took quite a long time to get at . . .' In reference to this procedure of approach, Wemmick suggests that 'It brushes the Newgate cobwebs away . . .' although he fails to recognize that he has verbally re-drawn the walls of his own narrowed life. William Dorrit is 'a very different man from the doctor, but he had already begun to travel, by his opposite segment of the circle, to the same point' (*Little Dorrit* Book 1, chapter 6) and the illustration by Browne of 'The Pensioner Entertainment' defies one to recognize the homely warmth of tea-time comfort as being the inside of a prison.

The suspension of transportation in 1853 meant that prison sentences became longer, and in Foucault's analysis the model prison became a means of reducing prisoners to the state when they will recognize the reforming ideals of the penitentiary within their own minds: incarceration is accepted and internalized. With the observation post of panoptical architecture keeping surveillance over the inmates, like Nadgett the detective in *Martin Chuzzlewit* who knows everything about everybody, the only hiding-place is in a world of fictional invention, a world inside one's own mind. Although, as Mrs Gamp says in chapter 19, 'we knows wot's hidden in each other's breasts and if we had glass winders there, we'd need to keep the shetters up, some on us, I do assure you.'

The long-term effects of imprisonment and the damaging conse-
quences to the human spirit were made movingly clear in Dickens's
comments on the Eastern Penitentiary, in chapter 7 of *American Notes*:

> In its intention, I am well convinced that it is kind, humane, and
> meant for reformation; but I am persuaded that those who devised
> this system of Prison Discipline, and those benevolent gentlemen
> who carry it into execution, do not know what it is that they are
> doing. I believe that very few men are capable of estimating the
> immense amount of torture and agony which this dreadful punish-
> ment, prolonged for years, inflicts upon the sufferers; and in guess-
> ing at it myself, and in reasoning from what I have seen written
> upon their faces, and what to my certain knowledge they feel
> within, I am only the more convinced that there is a depth of ter-
> rible endurance in it which none but the sufferers themselves can
> fathom, and which no man has a right to inflict upon his fellow
> creature. I hold this slow and daily tampering with the mysteries of
> the brain, to be immeasurably worse than any torture of the body:
> and because its ghastly signs and tokens are not so palpable to the
> eye and sense of touch as scars upon the flesh; because its wounds
> are not upon the surface, and it extorts few cries that human ears
> can hear; therefore I the more denounce it, as a secret punishment
> which slumbering humanity is not roused up to stay.

STUDY QUESTIONS

1. This chapter has focused on what Edgar Johnson termed
   'Dickens's life-long preoccupation with prison'. What other
   examples can you find in *Great Expectations* to support the view
   that prison is the dominant theme?
2. *Great Expectations* was the second novel in which Dickens used
   the first-person singular narrative technique. Have a close look at
   the first two chapters of *David Copperfield* and see what comparisons you can draw with the opening two chapters of the later novel.
3. Read 'George Silverman's Explanation', which you will find in
   the Oxford University Press volume of Dickens's work, *The
   Uncommercial Traveller and Reprinted Pieces*. Trace the theme of
   guilt in this story in terms of its echoing the feelings which Pip
   has in *Great Expectations*.

CHAPTER 3

READING *GREAT EXPECTATIONS*

PASSAGE 1

At the same time, he hugged his shuddering body in both his arms – clasping himself, as if to hold himself together – and limped towards the low church wall. As I saw him go, picking his way among the nettles, and among the brambles that bound the green mounds, he looked in my young eyes as if he were eluding the hands of the dead people, stretching up cautiously out of their graves, to get a twist upon his ankle and pull him in.

When he came to the low church wall, he got over it, like a man whose legs were numbed and stiff, and then turned round to look for me. When I saw him turning, I set my face towards home, and made the best use of my legs. But presently I looked over my shoulder, and saw him going on again towards the river, still hugging himself in both arms, and picking his way with his sore feet among the great stones dropped into the marshes here and there, for stepping-places when the rains were heavy, or the tide was in.

The marshes were just a long black horizontal line then, as I stopped to look after him; and the river was just another horizontal line, not nearly so broad nor yet so black; and the sky was just a row of long angry red lines and dense black lines intermixed. On the edge of the river I could faintly make out the only two black things in all the prospect that seemed to be standing upright; one of these was the beacon by which the sailors steered – like an unhooped cask upon a pole – an ugly thing when you were near it; the other a gibbet, with some chains hanging to it which had once held a pirate. The man was limping on towards this latter, as if he were the pirate come to life, and come down, and going back to hook himself up again. It gave me a terrible turn when I thought so; and as I saw the cattle lifting their heads to gaze after him, I wondered whether they thought so too. I looked all round for the horrible young man, and could see no signs of him. But now I was frightened again, and ran home without stopping.

(chapter 1, pp. 6–7)

This passage from the end of chapter 1 emphasizes the associations Pip feels between himself and the convict, as well as highlighting the fears felt by a vulnerable young boy who feels himself isolated. As the convict 'limped' towards the wall, we are given a foretaste of Pip's difficulties as he keeps the hidden piece of bread down his trouser leg and the 'hands of the dead people' act as a reminder of the conscience which strains to pull Pip down. As opposed to limping, Pip 'made the best use' of his legs in going home, but here again there is a contrasting association with the convict: in chapter 5 he recalls being associated with 'a fierce young hound' if he joins the hunt for the convict. The use of the word 'bound' in terms of the nettles and brambles echoes what becomes for Pip a restriction upon his future aspirations which is also associated with crime. In chapter 3, as he searches in the cold morning for the escaped convict, 'I couldn't warm my feet, to which the damp cold seemed riveted, as the iron was riveted to the leg of the man I was running to meet' and he knows his way to the Battery because he had been there with Joe, who had told him that when he was apprenticed he would be 'regularly bound'. The criminal emphasis associated with 'bound' is further explored in chapter 13 when Pumblechook announces that 'This boy must be bound out of hand'. He then repeats the sentiment with a sense of glee:

'A pleasure's a pleasure all the world over. But this boy, you know; we must have him bound.'

(p. 104)

When he is then taken to the Town Hall to be 'bound apprentice to Joe in the Magisterial presence', he feels 'exactly as if I had that moment picked a pocket or fired a rick'. Pumblechook holds him 'all the while as if we had looked in on our way to the scaffold'. Further associations between Pip and the criminal world are hinted at in the reference to the executed pirate who appears to have come down and is now returning to 'hook himself up again'. After the prisoners have been retaken and Pip and Joe have returned to the Forge in chapter 6, Mrs Joe takes Pip to bed in such a manner as to suggest his being hauled up the gallows: she 'assisted me up to bed with such a strong hand that I seemed to have fifty boots on and to be dangling them all against the edges of the stairs.' There is a similar criminal association when Pip first visits Miss Havisham at Satis House in chapter 8. When Pip has finished his card game with Estella, Miss Havisham, acting the rôle of judge, says 'Estella, take him down. Let him have something to eat, and let him roam and look about him while he eats.' With the echo of the pirate who has 'come to life, and come down', Pip is identified here with Magwitch when he is eating the stolen food in chapter 3:

> He swallowed, or rather snapped up, every mouthful, too soon and too fast; and he looked sideways here and there while he ate, as if he thought there was danger in every direction of some-body's coming to take the pie away.
>
> (p. 19)

The association which Pip feels between himself and the criminal world is further highlighted in chapter 15 when Mr Wopsle is reading 'the affecting tragedy of George Barnwell' who had been 'running to seed, leaf after leaf, ever since his course began', and the association between 'Pip' and 'seed' suggests a career which is destined for prison since, as Mrs Joe told him in chapter 2, felons always begin their careers by robbing, forging and asking questions. At that point Pip 'felt fearfully sensible of the great convenience that the hulks were handy for me.'

Images of being captured or trapped and slaughtered reappear in the early chapters of the novel. At their first meeting, in chapter 1, Magwitch threatened to eat Pip: '"You young dog," said the man, licking his lips, "what fat cheeks you ha' got."' He then terrifies the boy by telling him of the young associate of his who 'has a secret way pecooliar to himself, of getting at a boy, and at his heart, and at his liver.' At the Christmas dinner on the following day, Pumblechook refers to Pip as a pig, and suggests that

> 'You would have been disposed of for so many shillings according to the market price of the article, and Dunstable the butcher would have come up to you as you lay in your straw, and he would have whipped you under his left arm, and with his right he would have tucked up his frock to get a penknife from out of his waistcoat-pocket, and he would have shed your blood and had your life.'
>
> (p. 27)

This particular position has already held Pip when Mrs Joe administers the tar-water in chapter 2:

> On this particular evening, the urgency of my case demanded a pint of this mixture, which was poured down my throat, for my greater comfort, while Mrs. Joe held my head under her arm, as a boot would be held in a boot-jack.
>
> (p. 12)

Pip's association with the criminal world is also highlighted by the way in which he runs out of the house at the end of chapter 4

> head foremost into a party of soldiers with their muskets: one of whom held out a pair of handcuffs to me, saying, 'Here you are, look sharp, come on!'
>
> (p. 30)

When the party sets out in pursuit of the convicts, Pip whispers 'treasonably' to Joe that he hopes that they won't find them.

The association between being a gentleman and being a criminal is first raised by Magwitch as he clutches onto Compeyson in chapter 5: 'He's a gentleman, if you please, this villain. Now, the Hulks has got its gentleman again, through me.' Pip's imprisoning connection with Magwitch is then further cemented by the secret signal of complicity which passes between them:

> I had alighted from Joe's back on the brink of the ditch when we came up, and had not moved since. I looked at him eagerly when

he looked at me, and slightly moved my hands and shook my head. I had been waiting for him to see me, that I might try to assure him of my innocence.

(p. 38)

Chapter 5 ends with the torches being 'flung hissing into the water' and going out 'as if it were all over with him.' However, as chapter 6 opens, Pip recognizes the taint of what is left behind from the experience and his fear of losing Joe's confidence leads him into being 'too cowardly to do what I knew to be right, as I had been too cowardly to avoid doing what I knew to be wrong.' Like the 'hands of the dead people' in this passage, which seem to stretch 'out of their graves, to get a twist upon his ankle and pull him in', the past will haunt Pip like an irremovable stain.

PASSAGE 2

Behind the furthest end of the brewery, was a rank garden with an old wall: not so high but that I could struggle up and hold on long enough to look over it, and see that the rank garden was the garden of the house, and that it was overgrown with tangled weeds, but that there was a track upon the green and yellow paths, as if someone sometimes walked there, and that Estella was walking away from me even then. But she seemed to be everywhere. For, when I yielded to the temptation presented by the casks, and began to walk on them, I saw her walking on them at the end of the yard of casks. She had her back towards me, and held her pretty brown hair spread out in her two hands, and never looked round, and passed out of my view directly. So, in the brewery itself – by which I mean the large paved lofty place in which they used to make the beer, and where the brewing utensils still were. When I first went into it, and, rather oppressed by its gloom, stood near the door looking about me, I saw her pass among the extinguished fires, and ascend some light iron stairs, and go out by a gallery high overhead, as if she were going out into the sky.

It was in this place, and at this moment, that a strange thing happened to my fancy. I thought it a strange thing then, and I thought it a stranger thing long afterwards. I turned my eyes – a little dimmed by looking up at the frosty light – towards a great wooden beam in a low nook of the building near me on my right hand, and I saw a figure hanging there by the neck. A figure all in yellow white, but with one shoe to the feet; and it hung so, that I could see that the faded trimmings of the dress were like earthy paper, and that the face was Miss Havisham's with a movement going over the whole countenance as if she were trying to call to me. In the terror of seeing the figure, and in the terror of being certain that it had not been there a moment before, I at first ran from it, and then ran towards it. And my terror was greatest of all when I found no figure there.

(chapter 8, p. 64)

This passage from Pip's first visit to Satis House gives us a glimpse into a phantasmagorical world that has eerie associations with both crime and imprisonment, as well as hinting at the unobtainable quality of social aspirations. When Satis House is first mentioned in chapter 7, it is as a 'large and dismal house barricaded against robbers.' The 'rank garden with an old wall' finds a later counterpart in the visit to Newgate prison in chapter 32, where Wemmick 'walked among the prisoners, much as a gardener might walk among his plants.' In this passage, the nervous Pip looks over the wall and obtains a dreamlike glimpse of another world 'overgrown with tangled weeds' but having a 'track upon the green and yellow paths.' The dreamlike sense of distance adds to the unobtainable quality of the star-like Estella who passes 'among the extinguished fires' to 'ascend some light iron stairs', before disappearing 'as if she were going out into the sky.'

The cold distance conjured up by stars (stella) is a measure of the social gap felt by Pip and is further emphasized by the reference to 'looking up at the frosty light.' The tightly woven structure of this novel can be seen here as the reader recalls the evening that Mrs Joe and Pumblechook arrive home with the news that Miss Havisham wants a boy to go and play at Satis House. As Pip and Joe listen at the door for the chaise-cart to return on market-day, it is 'a dry cold night, and the wind blew keenly, and the frost was white and hard.' The pitiless nature of the weather puts Pip in mind of the convict:

A man would die to-night of lying out on the marshes, I thought. And then I looked at the stars, and considered how awful it would be for a man to turn his face up to them as he froze to death, and see no help or pity in all the glittering multitude.

(p. 50)

The reappearance of the hanging figure from the gallows in passage confirms the haunting quality which surrounds the frightened Pip. A 'figure hanging there by the neck' suggests a gibbet and the 'yellow white' clothes echo Pip's first sight of Miss Havisham in her 'withered bridal dress' and 'grave-clothes', with the 'long veil so like a shroud.' This deathly quality of the vision is further noted in the dress being 'like earthy paper'. The theme of the physical aspects associated with hanging are reproduced in a semi-comic fashion in chapter 11 with the description of Camilla, Miss Havisham's relative, who tells of the 'nervous jerkings I have in my legs'. These 'chokings and nervous jerkings' are said by Camilla to be uncontrol-lable offshoots of her great love for her relative. This affection is, however, little more than greed and a desire for 'great expectations' on Miss Havisham's decease. To emphasize the choking image, Camilla later 'put her hand to her throat'. For the hanging figure to seem to be 'trying to call to me' suggests the beckoning sense of criminal intrigue and, as with his dealings with Magwitch at the start of the novel, he 'at first ran from it' and then 'ran towards it'. The magnetic attraction of social climbing, 'great expectations' is some-thing to be both shunned and pursued: its gains will not exceed the losses incurred in obtaining them.

That Satis House is connected to the theme of crime in the novel is evident from the opening of chapter 8:

> Within a quarter of an hour we came to Miss Havisham's house, which was of old brick, and dismal, and had a great many iron bars to it. Some of the windows had been walled up; of those that remained, all the lower were rustily barred . . .
>
> (p. 55)

Pursuing the image of a prison, Pip is let in by a young lady 'with keys in her hand', who locks the gate after he has entered. On his entrance, Pip is greeted by a haunting recollection of the marsh scene with the hulks at the start of the novel:

> The cold wind seemed to blow colder there, than outside the gate; and it made a shrill noise in howling in and out at the open sides of the brewery, like the noise of wind in the rigging of a ship at sea.
>
> (p. 56)

Estella escorts Pip along passages that 'were all dark' and 'we went through more passages and up a staircase, and still it was all dark, and only the candle lighted us.' The fantastical atmosphere of the place as it is evoked here is further explored in chapter 11 in Pip's second visit to Satis House when he discovers a gate in the garden which he had not seen before through which he enters 'a wilderness'. Here he is confronted by the young Herbert Pocket who challenges him to a fight. Pip's bloody victory over the 'pale young gentleman' gives him little satisfaction:

Indeed, I go so far as to hope that I regarded myself while dressing, as a species of savage young wolf, or other wild beast.

(pp. 92–3)

Inevitably, this language echoes that which Dickens uses in reference to the earlier fight between Magwitch and the 'gentleman' Compeyson:

'Here are both men!' panted the sergeant, struggling at the bottom of a ditch. 'Surrender, you two! and confound you for two wild beasts! Come asunder.'

(p. 36)

In the earlier fight, Compeyson was defeated by Magwitch: 'The other convict was livid to look at, and, in addition to the old bruised left side of his face, seemed to be bruised and torn all over.' His accusation against Magwitch is that 'he tried to murder me'. The fight in Miss Havisham's garden, while being presented in a comic light, has an undercurrent of brutality to it:

He got heavily bruised, for I am sorry to record that the more I hit him, the harder I hit him; but he came up again and again and again, until at last he got a bad fall with the back of his head against the wall.

(p. 92)

The shed blood stains Pip's trousers and he tries to wash out 'that evidence of my guilt in the dead of night', and the recurring stain is emphasized only a few lines later by his attempt to cover 'the traces of gore in that spot' with 'garden-mould from the eye of man.' This violence in which Pip is involved is a step along the road of associations which will make him feel guilty for the murderous attack upon his sister which is referred to in chapter 16. Not only has he already been associated in the eyes of Pumblechook with the criminal George Barnwell, but he has also been stared at by the seed-merchant 'as if it were a well-known fact that I contemplated murdering a near relation'. He is also associated with the attack upon Mrs Joe, since the weapon used appears to be the convict's leg-iron which Pip had helped, by his theft of a file, to cut asunder.

It was horrible to think that I had provided the weapon, however undesignedly, but I could hardly think otherwise.

(p. 121)

The association with Barnwell refers to George Lillo's play, *The London Merchant,or, the History of George Barnwell*, first performed in 1731. In this domestic tragedy, a young apprentice is seduced by Sarah Millwood, whom he loves, into robbing his master and murdering his uncle. In the play, both Millwood and Barnwell end up on the gallows. As with the reappearance of the file in chapter 10 when the stranger in the Jolly Bargemen stirs his rum-and-water, the introduction of the leg-iron serves as a reminder of the impossibility of Pip's ever being able to shake off the past.

PASSAGE 3

It is a most miserable thing to feel ashamed of home. There may be black ingratitude in the thing, and the punishment may be retributive and well-deserved; but, that it is a miserable thing, I can testify.

Home had never been a very pleasant place to me, because of my sister's temper. But, Joe had sanctified it, and I believed in it. I had believed in the best parlour as a most elegant saloon; I had believed in the front door, as a mysterious portal of the Temple of State whose solemn opening was attended with a sacrifice of roast fowls; I had believed in the kitchen as a chaste though not magnificent apartment; I had believed in the forge as the glowing road to manhood and independence. Within a single year all this was changed. Now, it was all coarse and common, and I would not have had Miss Havisham and Estella see it on any account.

How much of my ungracious condition of mind may have been my own fault, how much Miss Havisham's, how much my sister's, is now of no moment to me or to any one. The change was made in me; the thing was done. Well or ill done, excusably or inexcusably, it was done.

Once, it had seemed to me that when I should at last roll up my shirt-sleeves and go into the forge, Joe's 'prentice, I should be distinguished and happy. Now the reality was in my hold, I only felt that I was dusty with the dust of the small coal, and that I had a weight upon my daily remembrance to which the anvil was a feather. There have been occasions in my later life (I suppose as in most lives) when I have felt for a time as if a thick curtain had fallen on all its interest and romance, to shut me out from anything save dull endurance any more. Never has that curtain dropped so heavy and blank, as when my way in life lay stretched out straight before me through the newly-entered road of apprenticeship to Joe.

I remember that at a later period of my 'time', I used to stand about the churchyard on Sunday evenings, when night was falling, comparing my own perspective with the windy marsh view, and making out some likeness between them by thinking how flat and low both were, and how on both there came an unknown way and a dark mist and then the sea. I was quite as dejected on the first working-day of my apprenticeship as in that after-time; but I am glad to know that I never breathed a murmur to Joe while my indentures lasted. It is about the only thing I *am* glad to know of myself in that connexion.

(chapter 14, pp. 106–7)

The original running head on the right-hand page of chapter 14 in the 1867 Charles Dickens Edition reads 'I am ill at ease in my mind'. The shame which is felt by Pip had been registered in the previous chapter when Joe had been at Satis House, where he had been asked to present Pip's indentures:

> I am afraid I was ashamed of the dear good fellow – I know I was ashamed of him – when I saw that Estella stood at the back of Miss Havisham's chair, and that her eyes laughed mischievously.
>
> (p. 101)

The description of the manner in which Pip had viewed his home has a quality of reverence and affection, belief and security, all of which are lost as 'the curtain dropped so heavy and blank', as though that stage of life was over. The reverence is suggested by the accumulation of 'sanctified', 'believed in it', 'mysterious portal', 'Temple', 'solemn' and 'sacrifice'. The central attribute of one's home forming the foundation of what one might go on to achieve is placed in terms which are serious and sober, with 'belief in the forge' leading to 'the glowing road to manhood and independence.' That belief has been tainted and Pip is exiled by his perception that 'it was all coarse and common'. That the theme of the lost home is central to the novel is emphasized after Magwitch has been captured in chapter 55 and Pip returns to his lodgings. He has the example before him of the modest domesticity which informs the relationship between Herbert Pocket and Clara and he then 'went to my lonely home – if it deserved the name, for it was now no home to me, and I had no home anywhere.' The sense of shame which he feels is connected to social aspirations, and when he wonders how much the fault may lie with himself, Miss Havisham or his sister he may well recall Mrs Joe's greeting when he and Joe returned from Satis House in the previous chapter:

'And what's happened to you? I wonder you condescend to come back to such poor society as this, I am sure I do.'

(p. 103)

Pip's visits to the other world of Satis House have left their own stain upon his life, as he had already recognized in chapter 12:

What could I become with these surroundings? How could my character fail to be influenced by them? Is it to be wondered at if my thoughts were dazed, as my eyes were, when I came out into the natural light from the misty yellow rooms?

(p. 96)

The fear of Miss Havisham and, even more, Estella peering into Pip's coarse life as an apprenticed blacksmith is heightened later on in chapter 14 when Pip imagines the girl's eyes scorning him:

Often after dark, when I was pulling the bellows for Joe, and we were singing Old Clem, and when the thought how we used to sing it at Miss Havisham's would seem to show me Estella's face in the fire, with her pretty hair fluttering in the wind and her eyes scorning me, – often at such a time I would look towards those panels of black night in the wall which the wooden windows then were, and would fancy that I saw her just drawing her face away.

(p. 108)

The imagery of imprisonment is heightened by the fact that blacksmiths' forges had glassless windows secured by wooden bars.

What I dreaded was, that in some unlucky hour I, being at my grimiest and commonest, should lift up my eyes and see Estella looking in at one of the wooden windows of the forge. I was haunted by the fear that she would, sooner or later, find me out, with a black face and hands, doing the coarsest part of my work, and would exult over me and despise me.

(p. 108)

The emphasis upon being found out echoes the being 'beggared' by Estella in the card game on his first visit to Satis House, and the sense of being observed may well echo the author's feelings of being on display in the window of the Covent Garden blacking warehouse. John Dickens's quarrel with his son's employer may have been based upon the public nature of the employment and with his son being recognized as a common workman. In the autobiographical extracts quoted by Forster, Dickens suggests that the quarrel 'may have had some backward reference, in part, for anything I know, to my employment at the window' (Forster, p. 26).

The idea of the light going out, 'the glowing road' changing, 'a thick curtain' falling on interest and romance making life something of 'dull endurance' echoes earlier images. When Pip feels ashamed of the lies he has told about his visit to Miss Havisham he goes to the Forge in chapter 9 to confess to Joe with the words 'Before the fire goes out, Joe, I should like to tell you something'. That the light of the forge should remain a powerful image of security and simple happiness for Pip is felt when he is living in London having started on his road to becoming a gentleman:

> When I woke up in the night – like Camilla – I used to think, with a weariness in my spirits, that I should have been happier and better if I had never seen Miss Havisham's face, and had risen to manhood content to be partners with Joe in the honest old forge. Many a time of an evening, when I sat alone looking at the fire, I thought, after all, there was no fire like the forge fire and the kitchen fire at home.
>
> (p. 272)

There is an ominous tone to this since the first visit to Satis House, acting as a counterpart to the experience with the convict on the marshes, has a lasting effect on Pip's life. Whereas with the former 'the torches were flung hissing into the water, and went out, as if it were all over with him', now the first steps on the journey of exile from home have been taken:

> Pause you who read this, and think for a moment of the long chain of iron or gold, of thorns or flowers, that would never have bound you, but for the formation of the first link on one memorable day.
>
> (p. 72)

The association of 'chain' with imprisonment is further emphasized when Joe wonders whether Pip might make a gift for Miss
Havisham: 'a new chain for the front door', 'a gross or two of shark-
headed screws', 'a toasting-fork' or 'a gridiron'. The image of honest
hard work which brings the workingman its own reward is suggested
in the picture of Pip rolling up his shirt-sleeves and going into the
forge. Joe had already said to Miss Havisham, via Pip, in reply to her
question as to whether the boy had any objections to being apprenticed to the trade of blacksmith, 'And there weren't no objection on
your part, and Pip it were the great wish of your hart.' The picture
was such as to make Pip 'distinguished and happy'. However, the
coarse reality is now perceived as 'dusty with the dust of the small
coal', the vulgar ordinariness of which had a precedent with the two
pound notes that the convict's friend had given him in chapter 10:
'two fat sweltering one-pound notes that seemed to have been on
terms of the warmest intimacy with all the cattle-markets in the
county.' As if to endorse this common payment for services ren-
dered, Miss Havisham insists upon Pip receiving a small financial
gift on his birthday:

> I tried to decline taking the guinea on the first occasion, but with
> no better effect than causing her to ask me very angrily, if I
> expected more? Then, and after that, I took it.
>
> (p. 127)

The association of dissatisfaction with home and alienation from
childhood's dreams with the appearance of the convict at the
opening of the novel is still felt as Pip stands 'about the churchyard
on Sunday evenings, when night was falling'. He recognizes the 'likeness' between his own perspective and the 'windy marsh view' in the
way he had identified himself with the convict and the hanged pirate.
Now, in his state of social self-despising he sees the connection as
'flat and low' and surrounded by 'a dark mist'.

PASSAGE 4

Biddy asked me here, as she sat holding my sister's plate, 'Have you thought about when you'll show yourself to Mr. Gargery, and your sister, and me? You will show yourself to us; won't you?'

'Biddy,' I returned with some resentment, 'you are so exceedingly quick that it's difficult to keep up with you.'

('She always were quick,' observed Joe.)

'If you had waited another moment, Biddy, you would have heard me say that I shall bring my clothes here in a bundle one evening – most likely on the evening before I go away.'

Biddy said no more. Handsomely forgiving her, I soon exchanged an affectionate good night with her and Joe, and went up to bed. When I had got into my little room, I sat down and took a long look at it, as a mean little room that I should soon be parted from and raised above, for ever. It was furnished with fresh young remembrances too, and even at the same moment I fell into much the same confused division of mind between it and the better rooms to which I was going, as I had been in so often between the forge and Miss Havisham's, and Biddy and Estella.

The sun had been shining brightly all day on the roof of my attic, and the room was warm. As I put the window open and stood looking out, I saw Joe come slowly forth at the dark door below, and take a turn or two in the air; and then I saw Biddy come, and bring him a pipe and light it for him. He never smoked so late, and it seemed to hint to me that he wanted comforting, for some reason or other.

He presently stood at the door immediately beneath me, smoking his pipe, and Biddy stood there too, quietly talking to him, and I knew that they talked of me, for I heard my name mentioned in an endearing tone by both of them more than once. I would not have listened for more, if I could have heard more: so, I drew away from the window, and sat down in my one chair by the bedside, feeling it very sorrowful and strange that this first night of my bright fortunes should be the loneliest I had ever known.

Looking towards the open window, I saw light wreaths from Joe's pipe floating there, and I fancied it was like a blessing from Joe – not obtruded on me or paraded before me, but pervading the air we shared together. I put my light out, and crept into bed; and it was an uneasy bed now, and I never slept the old sound sleep in it any more.

(chapter 18, pp. 145–6)

The importance of clothes in this passage goes to the heart of what it is to be a gentleman. Pip has already suggested, in chapter 18, that he will 'go down town on Monday' to order his new clothes and will then have them sent to Pumblechook's, since 'It would be very disagreeable to be stared at by all the people here.' Joe suggests that 'Mr. and Mrs. Hubble might like to see you in your new gen-teel figure too, Pip . . . So might Wopsle. And the Jolly Bargemen might take it as a compliment.' Bearing in mind the way Pip used to sit beside Joe 'whenever I entered that place of resort', and the way he 'fell into the space Joe made for me' there is a sense here of the public house acting as a homely extension of the Forge. The distance that Pip has travelled in his mind, and the alienation he now feels from the past is then echoed in the embarrassing criticism Pip offers: 'That's just what I don't want, Joe. They would make such a business of it – such a coarse and common business – that I couldn't bear myself.' There is a feeling of shame and subterfuge in Pip's use of the word 'bundle', as though his gentleman's appearance is something to be ashamed of. In chapter 19 after he had presented himself at Satis House in his new clothes, to the great discomfort of Sarah Pocket and therefore allowing himself unwittingly to be used by his 'fairy godmother', he returned to Pumblechook's house, 'took off my new clothes, made them into a bundle, and went back home in my older dress, carrying it – to speak the truth – much more at my ease too, though I had the bundle to carry.'

The connection between Pip's clothes and crime was first suggested when he is being washed and dressed by Mrs Joe in preparation for his first visit to Satis House:

When my ablutions were completed, I was put into clean linen of the stiffest character, like a young penitent into sackcloth, and was trussed up in my tightest and fearfullest suit. I was then delivered over to Mr. Pumblechook, who formally received me as if he were the sheriff . . .

(p. 53)

Imprisoned in these clothes like the inmate of a penitentiary, Pip says farewell to Joe in such a manner as to hint at the finality involved in such a separation: 'I had never parted from him before, and what with my feelings and what with soap-suds, I could at first see no stars from the chaise-cart.'

The imagery of clothes as borrowed or stolen items of superficial importance recurs when Pip is in London and finds himself introduced by a drunken 'minister of justice' to the yard in Newgate Prison where the gallows is kept. In a reminder of Pip's own felonious past he is informed that four criminals

> would come out at that door the day after to-morrow at eight in the morning to be killed in a row. This was horrible, and gave me a sickening idea of London: the more so as the Lord Chief Justice's proprietor wore (from his hat down to his boots and up again to his pocket-handkerchief inclusive) mildewed clothes, which had evidently not belonged to him originally, and which, I took it into my head, he had bought cheap of the executioner.
>
> (p. 166)

By contrast, when Pip meets Herbert Pocket in chapter 22 he is conscious that 'he carried off his rather old clothes, much better than I carried off my new suit.'

Pip's sharp retort to Biddy's direct question about when he will show himself off in his new clothes to Joe, Mrs Joe and herself, registers the annoyed embarrassment at having been discovered to associate his closest family with the 'coarse and common business'. His condescension in 'Handsomely forgiving her' is to be echoed at the opening of the next chapter when he goes to church with Joe and feels

> a sublime compassion for the poor creatures who were destined to go there, Sunday after Sunday, all their lives through, and to lie obscurely at last among the low green mounds. I promised myself that I would do something for them one of these days, and formed a plan in outline for bestowing a dinner of roast-beef and plum-pudding, a pint of ale, and a gallon of condescension, upon everybody in the village.
>
> (p. 147)

The distance that Pip has travelled in his attitude towards his home is then presented uncomfortably as he suggests to Joe that it is a pity he did not learn more from the educational opportunities offered to him and recognizes that if he were to do something for Joe's advancement 'it would have been much more agreeable if he had been better qualified for a rise in station.'

In the passage, as Pip hears Biddy and Joe talking about him 'in an endearing tone', he moves away from the window as if he doesn't wish to listen to any comments which would heighten the feeling of guilt he has at his sudden rise in fortune. However, he feels instead a great sense of loneliness at being cut adrift from that warm centre of home. The phrase 'sorrowful and strange' is taken up in the next chapter after Pip has had a disagreement with Biddy over the nature of pride and dignity:

> I went out at the garden gate and took a dejected stroll until supper-time; again feeling it very sorrowful and strange that this, the second night of my bright fortunes, should be as lonely and unsatisfactory as the first.
>
> (p. 150)

The awareness of what he has lost lingers in Pip's mind to the extent that when he has boarded the coach for London he

> deliberated with an aching heart whether I would not get down when we changed horses and walk back, and have another evening at home, and a better parting.
>
> (p. 160)

Towards the end of the passage there is a contrast between the 'open window', the 'light wreaths' and the image of a blessing from Joe and that of Pip who 'crept into bed' which was 'uneasy'. The sense of a time passing which is never to be restored is movingly held in the finality of 'I never slept the old sound sleep in it any more.'

PASSAGE 5

Mr. Jaggers's room was lighted by a skylight only, and was a most dismal place; the skylight, eccentrically patched like a broken head, and the distorted adjoining houses looking as if they had twisted themselves to peep down at me through it. There were not so many papers about, as I should have expected to see; and there were some odd objects about, that I should not have expected to see – such as an old rusty pistol, a sword in a scabbard, several strange-looking boxes and packages, and two dreadful casts on a shelf, of faces peculiarly swollen, and twitchy about the nose. Mr. Jaggers's own high-backed chair was of deadly black horse-hair, with rows of brass nails round it, like a coffin; and I fancied I could see how he leaned back in it, and bit his forefinger at the clients. The room was but small, and the clients seemed to have had a habit of backing up against the wall; the wall, especially opposite to Mr. Jaggers's chair, being greasy with shoulders. I recalled too, that the one-eyed gentleman had shuffled forth against the wall when I was the innocent cause of his being turned out.

I sat down in the cliental chair placed over against Mr. Jaggers's chair, and became fascinated by the dismal atmosphere of the place. I called to mind that the clerk had the same air of knowing something to everybody else's disadvantage, as his master had. I wondered how many other clerks there were up-stairs, and whether they all claimed to have the same detrimental mastery of their fellow-creatures. I wondered what was the history of all the odd litter about the room, and how it came there. I wondered whether the two swollen faces were of Mr. Jaggers's family, and, if he were so unfortunate as to have had a pair of such ill-looking relations, why he stuck them on that dusty perch for the blacks and flies to settle on, instead of giving them a place at home. Of course I had no experience of a London summer day, and my spirits may have been oppressed by the hot exhausted air, and by the dust and grit that lay thick on everything. But I sat wondering and waiting in Mr. Jaggers's close room, until I really could not bear the two casts on the shelf above Mr. Jaggers's chair, and got up and went out.

(chapter 20, pp. 164–5)

The claustrophobic and gloomy atmosphere of Mr Jaggers's room in the offices of Little Britain is created by its surroundings as well as by its interior. Bartholomew Close and Little Britain were close to Smithfield, Newgate and Cheapside. The open market at Smithfield was the principal live cattle and horse market in London until 1852, and the present Old Bailey Central Criminal Court is built on the site of the old Newgate Prison. Pip's arrival at Cheapside earlier on in chapter 20 is at a world which is 'ugly, crooked, narrow, and dirty', and when he reaches Smithfield it is a 'shameful place, being all asmear with filth and fat and blood and foam' which 'seemed to stick to me'.

The lawyer's room is dominated by the 'two dreadful casts on a shelf', and in chapter 24 Wemmick informs Pip of their origin:

> These are two celebrated ones. Famous clients of ours that got us a world of credit. This chap (why you must have come down in the night and been peeping into the inkstand, to get this blot upon your eyebrow, you old rascal!) murdered his master, and, considering that he wasn't brought up to evidence, didn't plan it badly.
>
> (p. 200)

The story has an unnerving association with Pip who deserted his master, Joe, and attempted to bury the past in his pursuit of social standing. The second cast belongs to an executed criminal who 'forged wills' and was, in Wemmick's terms, 'a gentlemanly Cove'. Both terms have an uncomfortable association with Pip since he has not only inherited the wealth of a convicted criminal, but also risen in the world to become a 'gentleman'. Magwitch's partner, Compeyson, had 'set up fur a gentleman' and when Magwitch is first introduced to him he has the appearance of being 'a dab at the ways of gentlefolks':

> He has a watch and a chain and a ring and a breast-pin and a handsome suit of clothes.
>
> (p. 347)

The association between the 'dreadful cast' and the world of the gentleman is further emphasized when Magwitch tells Pip in chapter 42 that 'Compeyson's business was the swindling, handwriting forging, stolen bank-note passing, and such-like.'

Pip's feeling of being scrutinized by these heads reappears in chapter 48 when he is waiting in the office for Mr Jaggers and the rising and falling flame of the fire

> made the two casts on the shelf look as if they were playing a diabolical game at bo-peep with me; while the pair of coarse fat office-candles that dimly lighted Mr. Jaggers as he wrote in a corner, were decorated with dirty winding-sheets, as if in remembrance of a host of hanged clients.
>
> (p. 388)

In chapter 32, while waiting to meet Estella, Pip recognizes the 'taint' of prison which has surrounded his own social advance:

> I consumed the whole time in thinking how strange it was that I should be encompassed by all this taint of prison and crime; that, in my childhood out on our lonely marshes on a winter evening I should have first encountered it; that, it should have reappeared on two occasions, starting out like a stain that was faded but not gone; that, it should in this new way pervade my fortune and advancement.
>
> (p. 264)

The association, of course, heightens the gap which Pip feels between himself and the distant Estella, and he thinks 'with absolute abhorrence of the contrast between the jail and her' wishing that he hadn't met Wemmick first 'so that, of all the days in the year on this day, I might not have had Newgate in my breath and on my clothes.' As he goes to meet Estella he feels 'contaminated' and 'beat the prison dust off my feet' and 'shook it out of my dress'. When Pip had felt ashamed of his home in chapter 14 he had felt that he 'was dusty with the dust of the small coal' and now, in London, he feels the prison-like air oppressing him with 'the dust and grit that lay thick on everything'.

The 'dismal atmosphere' of the lawyer's room is exacerbated by the feeling Pip has of being watched by 'the distorted adjoining houses looking as if they had twisted themselves to peep down at me', and he feels that 'the clerk had the same air of knowing something to everybody else's disadvantage' which links back to Pip's feelings of guilt at the original theft of the food and file which opened the novel:

> Conscience is a dreadful thing when it accuses man or boy; but when, in the case of a boy, that secret burden co-operates with another secret burden down the leg of his trousers, it is (as I can testify) a great punishment.
>
> (pp. 12–13)

Here, even the word 'testify' has a legal ring to it. Mr Jaggers's conversation upholds this sense of claiming 'detrimental mastery' over other people when even his creaking boots 'laughed in a dry and suspicious way' recalling the original theft where 'every board upon the way, and every crack in every board' seems to call after Pip, 'Stop thief!' Wemmick even refers to Jaggers's manner as if 'he had set a man-trap and was watching it. Suddenly – click – you're caught!' This feeling of unease is further heightened by the confined nature of the room which forces clients into the habit of 'backing up against the wall'. These criminal associations of this room are further suggested by the 'old rusty pistol' and 'a sword in a scabbard' and Mr Jaggers's 'own high-backed chair' conveys an association with the death-sentence: 'deadly black horse-hair, with rows of brass nails round it, like a coffin'.

The association Pip feels with crime and execution and the inability of escaping from the past takes a further twist when he is accompanied by Wemmick to Barnard's Inn, 'a melancholy little square that looked to me like a flat burying-ground':

> A frouzy mourning of soot and smoke attired this forlorn creation of Barnard, and it had stewed ashes on its head, and was undergoing penance and humiliation as a mere dust-hole.
>
> (p. 173)

When he tries to open a window in the room he nearly executes himself, 'for the lines had rotted away, and it came down like a guillotine.'

PASSAGE 6

The time so melted away, that our early dinner-hour drew close at hand, and Estella left us to prepare herself. We had stopped near the centre of the long table, and Miss Havisham, with one of her withered arms stretched out of the chair, rested that clenched hand upon the yellow cloth. As Estella looked back over her shoulder before going out of the door, Miss Havisham kissed that hand to her, with a ravenous intensity that was of its kind quite dreadful.

Then, Estella being gone and we two left alone, she turned to me and said in a whisper:

'Is she beautiful, graceful, well-grown? Do you admire her?'

'Everybody must who sees her, Miss Havisham.'

She drew an arm round my neck, and drew my head close down to hers as she sat in the chair. 'Love her, love her, love her! How does she use you?'

Before I could answer (if I could have answered so difficult a question at all), she repeated, 'Love her, love her, love her! If she favours you, love her. If she wounds you, love her. If she tears your heart to pieces – and as it gets older and stronger it will tear deeper – love her, love her!'

Never had I seen such passionate eagerness as was joined to her utterance of these words. I could feel the muscles of the thin arm round my neck, swell with the vehemence that possessed her.

'Hear me, Pip! I adopted her to be loved. I bred her and educated her, to be loved. I developed her into what she is, that she might be loved. Love her!'

She said the word often enough, and there could be no doubt that she meant to say it; but if the often repeated word had been hate instead of love – despair – revenge – dire death – it could not have sounded from her lips more like a curse.

'I'll tell you,' she said, in the same hurried passionate whisper, 'what real love is. It is blind devotion, unquestioning self-humiliation, utter submission, trust and belief against yourself and against the whole world, giving up your whole heart and soul to the smiter – as I did!'

When she came to that, and to a wild cry that followed that, I caught her round the waist. For she rose up in the chair, in her

shroud of a dress, and struck at the air as if she would as soon
have struck herself against the wall and fallen dead.

(chapter 29, pp. 239–40)

This passage revolves around the witch-like qualities of Miss
Havisham and the consuming nature of her desire for revenge on
men for the manner in which she had been treated by Compeyson.
When she gloats over her creation of Estella, saying 'I bred her and
educated her, to be loved. I developed her into what she is, that she
might be loved', she anticipates the comments which appear later, in
chapter 38:

> 'How does she use you, Pip, how does she use you?' she asked me
> again, with her witch-like eagerness even in Estella's hearing.
>
> (p. 302)

In the sentence which precedes the main passage above in chapter 29
Pip felt, upon seeing Estella, that he 'was under stronger enchantment'. He sees his role as that of a chivalrous knight in Romance res-
cuing Sleeping Beauty; he is

> to restore the desolate house, admit the sunshine into the dark
> rooms, set the clocks a going and the cold hearths a blazing, tear
> down the cobwebs, destroy the vermin – in short, do all the
> shining deeds of the young Knight of romance, and marry the
> Princess.
>
> (p. 231)

However, in order to gain entrance to the castle and awaken the
Princess, he has to combat the 'seared red brick walls, blocked
windows, and strong green ivy clasping even the stacks of chimneys
with its twigs and tendons, as if with sinewy old arms'. He has also,
of course, to combat the newly acquired gatekeeper, Orlick, who has
been hired because there was no protection on the premises 'and it
come to be considered dangerous, with convicts and Tag and Rag
and Bobtail going up and down.'

The 'withered arms' and 'clenched hand' accompanied by 'a ravenous intensity' appear in that later chapter as 'the intensity of a
mind mortally hurt and diseased', as she sits with 'her other hand on

her crutch stick, and her chin on that, and her wan bright eyes glaring at me, a very spectre.' This witch-like imagery as it appears on Pip's first night that he stays at Satis House is suggestive of Lady Macbeth. Unable to rest at ease, Pip feels

> A thousand Miss Havishams haunted me. She was on this side of my pillow, on that, at the head of the bed, at the foot, behind the half-opened door of the dressing-room, in the dressing-room, in the room overhead, in the room beneath – everywhere.
>
> (p. 307)

Towards two o'clock in the morning he gets up to take a walk outside, but

> was no sooner in the passage than I extinguished my candle; for I saw Miss Havisham going along it in a ghostly manner, making a low cry. I followed her at a distance, and saw her go up the stair-case. She carried a bare candle in her hand, which she had prob-ably taken from one of the sconces in her own room, and was a most unearthly object by its light. Standing at the bottom of the staircase, I felt the mildewed air of the feast-chamber, without seeing her open the door, and I heard her walking there, and so across into her own room, and so across again into that, never ceasing the low cry.
>
> (p. 307)

The image from Macbeth is further suggested when Pip goes to dinner with Jaggers and meets Molly, Estella's mother:

> I cannot say whether any diseased affection of the heart caused her lips to be parted as if she were panting, and her face to bear a curious expression of suddenness and flutter; but I know that I had been to see Macbeth at the theatre, a night or two before, and that her face looked to me as if it were all disturbed by fiery air, like the faces I had seen rise out of the Witches' caldron.
>
> (p. 212)

In a further Shakespearian reference, the novel's concern with revenge is hinted at when Pip dreams of playing Hamlet to Miss

Havisham's Ghost. The revenge has a more pertinently relevant association for Pip when Miss Havisham is identified with Magwitch's
'young man hid with me' who 'has a secret way pecooliar to himself,
of getting at a boy, and at his heart, and at his liver.' This concern for
revenge prompts her to dwell on the phrase 'Love her', and to conjure
Pip to be so bound to this love that it will invade his very centre:

> 'If she wounds you, love her. If she tears your heart to pieces –
> and as it gets older and stronger it will tear deeper – love her, love
> her!'
>
> (p. 240)

When Pip takes Estella to Richmond in chapter 33, he recognizes
that 'It was impossible for me to avoid seeing that she cared to attract
me; that she made herself winning', and that this

> made me none the happier, for, even if she had not taken that tone
> of our being disposed of by others, I should have felt that she held
> my heart in her hand because she wilfully chose to do it, and not
> because it would have wrung any tenderness in her, to crush it and
> throw it away.
>
> (p. 270)

Pip's adoration of Estella is seen as a form of imprisonment, a
trap, and Herbert Pocket offers the advice to Pip that 'Not being
bound to her, can you not detach yourself from her?' Pip's reaction
to this suggestion brings the inescapable past looming into the
present 'like the old marsh winds coming up from the sea', and it
emphasizes his insecurity as he undergoes

> a feeling like that which had subdued me on the morning when I
> left the forge, when the mists were solemnly rising, and when I laid
> my hand upon the village finger-post . . .
>
> (p. 250)

Herbert points out to Pip that an inability to separate himself from
those early illusions 'may lead to miserable things'. This notwithstanding, Pip's answer is, of course, in the negative ('but I can't help
it'), and when Estella goes to live near the Green at Richmond with

Mrs Brandley, Pip 'suffered every kind and degree of torture that Estella could cause me.'

The Newgate contamination which Pip feels as he waits to meet Estella at the end of chapter 32 is taken up at the beginning of the next chapter, when she points out to him that

> 'We have no choice, you and I, but to obey our instructions. We are not free to follow our own devices, you and I.'
>
> (p. 265)

In contrast to the selfish motives which dominate the actions of Miss Havisham, when Pip decides that he wants to assist Herbert in business, he seeks the advice of Wemmick and is told that this sort of altruistic gesture of friendship has a cleansing effect:

> 'I thank you, for though we are strictly in our private and personal capacity, still it may be mentioned that there *are* Newgate cobwebs about, and it brushes them away.'
>
> (p. 296)

PASSAGE 7

It was wretched weather; stormy and wet, stormy and wet; and mud, mud, mud, deep in all the streets. Day after day, a vast heavy veil had been driving over London from the East, and it drove still, as if in the East there were an Eternity of cloud and wind. So furious had been the gusts, that high buildings in town had had the lead stripped off their roofs; and in the country, trees had been torn up, and sails of windmills carried away; and gloomy accounts had come in from the coast, of shipwreck and death. Violent blasts of rain had accompanied these rages of wind, and the day just closed as I sat down to read had been the worst of all.

Alterations had been made in that part of the Temple since that time, and it has not now so lonely a character as it had then, nor is it so exposed to the river. We lived at the top of the last house, and the wind rushing up the river shook the house that night, like discharges of cannon, or breakings of a sea. When the rain came with it and dashed against the windows, I thought, raising my eyes to them as they rocked, that I might have fancied myself in a storm-beaten lighthouse. Occasionally, the smoke came rolling down the chimney as though it could not bear to go out into such a night; and when I set the doors open and looked down the staircase, the staircase lamps were blown out; and when I shaded my face with my hands and looked through the black windows (opening them ever so little, was out of the question in the teeth of such wind and rain) I saw that the lamps on the bridges and the shore were shuddering and that the coal fires in barges on the river were being carried away before the wind like red-hot splashes in the rain.

I read with my watch upon the table, proposing to close my book at eleven o'clock. As I shut it, Saint Paul's, and all the many church-clocks in the City – some leading, some accompanying, some following – struck that hour. The sound was curiously flawed by the wind; and as I was listening, and thinking how the wind assailed and tore it, when I heard a footstep on the stair.

What nervous folly made me start, and awfully connect it with the footstep of my dead sister, matters not. It was past in a moment, and I listened again, and heard the footstep stumble in coming on. Remembering then, that the staircase lights were blown out, I took up my reading-lamp and went out to the stair-head. Whoever was below had stopped on seeing my lamp, for all was quiet.

'There is someone down there, is there not?' I called out, looking down.

'Yes,' said a voice from the darkness beneath.

'What floor do you want?'

'The top. Mr. Pip.'

'That is my name. – There is nothing the matter?'

'Nothing the matter,' returned the voice. And the man came on.

(chapter 39, pp. 313–14)

The running heads for the Charles Dickens Edition emphasize the importance of chapter 39: 'A stormy night in the Temple/I recognize my visitor/He explains my great mistake/And I wake from my dream'. The setting of the Temple is important since it was the only Inn of Court which had gardens running down to the Thames, and hence providing the first of many comparisons with the opening chapter of the novel where Pip is on the marshes which lie between Cooling churchyard and the Thames estuary. The dramatic importance of this scene where Magwitch returns, as it were from the dead, is heightened by the closing image of the 'Eastern story' which concluded the previous chapter:

In the Eastern story, the heavy slab that was to fall on the bed of state in the flush of conquest was slowly wrought out of the quarry, the tunnel for the rope to hold it in its place was slowly carried through the leagues of rock, the slab was slowly raised and fitted in the roof, the rope was rove to it and slowly taken through the miles of hollow to the great iron ring.

(p. 312)

The story referred to was No. 6 in *Tales of the Genii* (1764) by Sir Charles Morell (James Ridley), and it featured Misnar, the Sultan of India, whose wise vizier, Horam, destroyed his enemies by the construction of an elaborate trap. Dickens's fascination with the world of the collapsing ceiling was evidenced by his dramatizing this story as a child in one of the earliest of his writings.

The opening of the novel had found Pip alone in a graveyard 'on a memorable raw afternoon towards evening', and the landscape was like a 'distant savage lair from which the wind was rushing'. In passage 7, Pip is again alone since Herbert has gone to Marseilles on business and he is already feeling the absence of 'the cheerful face and ready response of my friend'. The action here also takes place as the day 'just closed', and the weather is suggestive of the portentous storm which will herald the ceiling falling in on Pip's expectations. The rushing wind of the first chapter finds a counterpart here with the 'wind rushing up the river', and the reference to the 'discharges of cannon' brings to mind the cannons firing their warning of convicts having escaped from the Hulks.

Whereas the marshes of the opening were a 'dark flat wilderness', here the 'staircase lamps' are blown out and Pip looks through 'the black windows', his isolation emphasized by the reference to fancying himself being 'in a storm-beaten lighthouse'. The haunting adventure surrounding the pursuit of the convicts in chapter 5 closed with 'the ends of the torches' being 'flung hissing in the water' extinguishing the episode, 'as if it were all over with him'. By comparison, here Pip sees that 'the coal fires in barges on the river were being carried away before the wind like red-hot splashes in the rain.' The dramatic elements of the description contain echoes of the night of Duncan's murder in *Macbeth* where Lennox describes how

> The night has been unruly. Where we lay
> Our chimneys were blown down, and, as they say,
> Lamentings heard i' th' air, strange screams of death,
> And prophesying with accents terrible
> Of dire combustion and confused events
> New-hatched to th' woeful time.
>
> (Act II, iii 53–8)

When Pip hears a footstep on the stair his immediate thought is to associate it with his dead sister, the attack upon whom is linked guiltily in his mind with the escaped convict since she had been hit with a broken fetter. His first reactions on hearing of Mrs Joe's death had been linked to her haunting him:

The figure of my sister in her chair by the kitchen fire, haunted me night and day. That the place could possibly be, without her, was something my mind seemed unable to compass; and whereas she had seldom or never been in my thoughts of late, I had now the strangest ideas that she was coming towards me in the street, or that she would presently knock at the door.

(p. 278)

The adult perspective on the fears which haunt the world of childhood, fears which have given the impression of being long buried, is caught with the phrase 'nervous folly'. The adult's reaction to the re-emergence of such fears is suggested by the phrase 'It was past in a moment'. An awareness that any visitor must be in need of a light prompts Pip to take up his reading-lamp and go to the stair-head. Just as Magwitch rose up from behind the graves in the opening chapter he rises again, as if from the dead, 'from the darkness beneath'. Like the ghost of Hamlet's murdered father, he is 'this fellow in the cellarage'. His inevitable arrival at 'the top', guided by the beacon of the light in Pip's hand, is emphasized with the brevity and directness of 'And the man came on.'

The theme of the reappearance of the convict is something which had haunted Dickens from his first major fiction and it is linked to the idea of the inescapable, the past which will never disappear. In *The Posthumous Papers of the Pickwick Club*, the digression in chapter 6 is 'The Story of The Convict's Return' and in a passage which has remarkable similarities with both the theme and the description in *Great Expectations*, John Edmunds 'stood before the old house – the home of his infancy – to which his heart had yearned with an intensity of affection not to be described, through long and weary years of captivity and sorrow'. As Edmunds stands outside what was his own childhood home, he 'felt the soft mild sleep of happy boyhood steal gently upon him'. However, the voices in the house 'fell strangely upon his ear; he knew them not'. In the last chapter of *Great Expectations*, Pip returns to the Forge after an absence of eleven years 'upon an evening in December, an hour or two after dark'. As he looks in 'unseen', he recognizes 'fenced into the corner with Joe's leg, and sitting on my own little stool looking into the fire' an image of himself. The mature and saddening recognition of the impossibility of ever going home is emphasized by Pip's hand upon the latch of the door, touching it 'so softly that I was not heard' and by the reference to Joe being 'a little grey'. The desire to return is inextricably linked with an acknowledgement of the impossibility of ever doing so.

Pip's identification with the convict, the exile who returns to seek his home, is recognized further on in chapter 39 when Magwitch is referred to as 'my convict':

> If the wind and the rain had driven away the intervening years, had scattered all the intervening objects, had swept us to the churchyard where we first stood face to face on such different levels, I could not have known my convict more distinctly than I knew him now, as he sat in the chair before the fire.
>
> (p. 316)

The unwanted family intimacy is realized when Magwitch 'caught me, drew me to the sofa, put me up against the cushions, and bent on one knee before me' and when a few lines later books and reading are referred to there is an image which parallels that of Wemmick reading to the Aged P. Pip's self-appointed father-figure tells him 'You shall read 'em to me, dear boy!'

PASSAGE 8

By the wilderness of casks that I had walked on long ago, and on which the rain of years had fallen since, rotting them in many places, and leaving miniature swamps and pools of water upon those that stood on end, I made my way to the ruined garden. I went all round it; round by the corner where Herbert and I had fought our battle; round by the paths where Estella and I had walked. So cold, so lonely, so dreary all!

Taking the brewery on my way back, I raised the rusty latch of a little door at the garden end of it, and walked through. I was going out at the opposite door – not easy to open now, for the damp wood had started and swelled, and the hinges were yielding, and the threshold was encumbered with a growth of fungus – when I turned my head to look back. A childish association revived with wonderful force in the moment of the slight action, and I fancied that I saw Miss Havisham hanging to the beam. So strong was the impression, that I stood under the beam shuddering from head to foot before I knew it was a fancy – though to be sure I was there in an instant.

The mournfulness of the place and time, and the great terror of this illusion, though it was but momentary, caused me to feel an indescribable awe as I came out between the open wooden gates where I had once wrung my hair after Estella had wrung my heart. Passing on into the front court-yard, I hesitated whether to call the woman to let me out at the locked gate, of which she had the key, or first to go up-stairs and assure myself that Miss Havisham was as safe and well as I had left her. I took the latter course and went up.

I looked into the room where I had left her, and I saw her seated in the ragged chair upon the hearth close to the fire, with her back towards me. In the moment when I was withdrawing my head to go quietly away, I saw a great flaming light spring up. In the same moment I saw her running at me, shrieking, with a whirl of fire blazing all about her, and soaring at least as many feet above her head as she was high.

(chapter 49, pp. 401–2)

The imagery of the first paragraph provides a convincing picture of the decaying effect of time and the desolation which reflects Pip's own feelings of disillusion. When Pip first visited Satis House and wandered round the 'rank garden' he had found a wall that was not 'so high but that I could struggle up and hold on long enough to look over it', and there is a sense of childish expectation in this peering into another world. However, here the tone of the writing is more bleakly dismal as if to record how the promises of youth have faded into the common light of day. The reference to the casks is followed by the glance backwards to when he had walked on them 'long ago' and the 'rain of years' combines the time passing with a dismal feeling of loss. The rottenness of the casks is accompanied by the stagnating quality of 'miniature swamps' and the reflective sense of deliberation in 'I made my way' raises the 'ruined garden' to become an image of the ruined heart. The echo here is of chapter 29 where Pip escorts Estella 'round the ruined garden twice or thrice more, and it was all in bloom for me'. On that occasion the 'green and yellow growth of weed in the chinks of the old wall' became for him 'the most precious flowers that ever blew', with that last word emphasizing the explosive and destructive nature of the affection. Pip's isolation is completed by the brief recollection of 'the corner where Herbert and I had fought our battle', since it brings to mind the quiet affection shared by Herbert and Clara as opposed to the wrecked ambitions of Pip who failed to reach his distant star, Estella.

The sense of decay is highlighted in the second paragraph with 'rusty latch', 'damp wood' yielding hinges and the 'growth of fungus', and the fantastical image of the gallows which has haunted Pip from the opening of the novel is reintroduced with the illusion of Miss Havisham 'hanging to the beam'. It is almost as if the Newgate stain is felt here and Wemmick's 'greenhouse' is an urban equivalent of this ruin:

> We were at Newgate in a few minutes, and we passed through the lodge where some fetters were hanging up on the bare walls among the prison rules, into the interior of the jail. At that time, jails were much neglected, and the period of exaggerated reaction consequent upon all public wrong-doing – and which is always its heaviest and longest punishment – was still far off.
>
> (p. 260)

When Wemmick shows Pip around the prison it is as though he 'walked among the prisoners, much as a gardener might walk among his plants'.

Pip first had the illusion of seeing Miss Havisham hanging from a beam on his initial visit to Satis House when he entered the web which had been spun for the punishment of men. He was keenly aware of being cruelly treated and vented his injured feelings by kicking a wall and twisting his own hair. The fantasy returns only after his eyes have been opened to the fact that nothing has come to him from Miss Havisham except unhappiness, and it is almost as if Pip's destructive sense of revenge is incorporated into the most extreme penalty of the law. Just as Orlick took Pip's revenge on Mrs Joe, legal judgement takes his revenge on Miss Havisham and it is interesting, perhaps, that both women die wishing to be pardoned.

The connection between Satis House and the world of imprisonment is further hinted at during Pip's tour of Newgate, with the reference to felons not being lodged and fed better than soldiers so that they 'seldom set fire to their prisons with the excusable object of improving the flavour of their soup'. This reference may well have been prompted by the riots at Chatham Prison in February 1861 and has an appropriateness here where fire will consume the barren years of waste. When Pip hesitates 'whether to call the woman to let me out at the locked gate, of which she had the key', it is almost as if he is seeking an exit from the prison which confines Miss Havisham both physically and psychologically. Wondering if he should 'first go up-stairs' to assure himself that Miss Havisham is safe, he could almost be Arthur Clennam in *Little Dorrit* mounting the stairs to Willam Dorrit's room in the Marshalsea.

The isolation felt by Pip is introduced at the start of this chapter which deals with the summons to Satis House. Pip goes down by coach to see Miss Havisham 'on a little matter of business', but he 'alighted at the Halfway House, and breakfasted there, and walked the rest of the distance' because of wishing 'to get into the town quietly by the unfrequented ways, and to leave it in the same manner'. The blighting of all his hopes is echoed in the fact that the 'best light of the day was gone', and as he passes the cathedral 'the swell of the old organ was borne to my ears like funeral music'. The figure of Miss Havisham is one of desolation as he sees her 'sitting on the hearth in a ragged chair, close before, and lost in contempla-

READING *GREAT EXPECTATIONS*

tion of, the ashy fire'. The 'air of utter loneliness' which surrounds her serves as a reminder that she is the spectral waste which has been consumed by vengeance and that with Estella now married she has no further part to play. The sense of decay is registered by Pip as he associates Miss Havisham with the extinction of light:

> That she had done a grievous thing in taking an impressionable child to mould into the form that her wild resentment, spurned affection, and wounded pride found vengeance in, I knew full well. But that, in shutting out the light of day, she had shut out infinitely more; that in seclusion, she had secluded herself from a thousand natural and healing influences; that her mind, brooding solitary, had grown diseased, as all minds do and must and will that reverse the appointed order of their Maker, I knew equally well.
>
> (p. 399)

PASSAGE 9

His breathing became more difficult and painful as the night drew on, and often he could not repress a groan. I tried to rest him on the arm I could use, in any easy position; but it was dreadful to think that I could not be sorry at heart for his being badly hurt, since it was unquestionably best that he should die. That there were, still living, people enough who were able and willing to identify him, I could not doubt. That he would be leniently treated, I could not hope. He who had been presented in the worst light at his trial, who had since broken prison and been tried again, who had returned from transportation under a life sentence, and who had occasioned the death of the man who was the cause of his arrest.

As we returned towards the setting sun we had yesterday left behind us, and as the stream of our hopes seemed all running back, I told him how grieved I was to think he had come home for my sake.

'Dear boy,' he answered, 'I'm quite content to take my chance. I've seen my boy, and he can be a gentleman without me.'

No. I had thought about that while we had been there side by side. No. Apart from any inclinations of my own, I understand Wemmick's hint now. I foresaw that, being convicted, his possessions would be forfeited to the Crown.

'Lookee here, dear boy,' said he. 'It's best as a gentleman should not be knowed to belong to me now. Only come to see me as if you come by chance alonger Wemmick. Sit where I can see you when I am swore to, for the last o' many times, and I don't ask no more.'

'I will never stir from your side,' said I, 'when I am suffered to be near you. Please God, I will be as true to you as you have been to me!'

I felt his hand tremble as it held mine, and he turned his face away as he lay in the bottom of the boat, and I heard that old sound in his throat – softened now, like all the rest of him. It was a good thing that he had touched this point, for it put into my mind what I might not otherwise have thought of until too late: that he need never know how his hopes of enriching me had perished.

(chapter 54, pp. 446–7)

Forster saw the pursuit of Magwitch on the river and his recapture as a counterpart to the opening chapter of the novel and recorded that Dickens had hired a steamer for the day from Blackwall to Southend 'To make himself sure of the actual course of a boat in such circumstances, and what possible incidents the adventure might have' (Forster, p. 569).

One of the most important lessons which Pip learns though the different stages of the novel is the value of friendship and loyalty. As he takes his place beside Magwitch in the four-oared galley which takes them back to London, he 'felt that that was my place henceforth while he lived.' Earlier in the chapter, Pip recognizes that he is setting out on a journey which draws a contrast with the one on which he set out so many years ago:

Of all my worldly possessions I took no more than the few necessaries that filled the bag.

(p. 434)

He also recognizes that his mind is 'wholly set on Provis's safety'. The loyalty which Magwitch has showed to Pip redeems some of the stain of the prison-house and this is recognized by the young man of 'great expectations' who had turned his back so easily on Joe Gargery:

For now my repugnance to him had all melted away, and in the hunted wounded shackled creature who held my hand in his, I only saw a man who had meant to be my benefactor, and who had felt affectionately, gratefully, and generously, towards me with great constancy through a series of years. I only saw in him a much better man than I had been to Joe.

(p. 446)

Pip faces up to the truth about the likelihood of Magwitch being condemned to death as a returned convict: returning from transportation remained a capital offence until 1834, although the last person to be hanged for this died in 1810. Ironically he now seems indeed to be like 'the pirate' from the opening chapter 'going back to hook himself up again'. This sense of the past's claim upon the present, the foiled ways of attempting to move forward into a new world, is emphasized with the return 'towards the setting sun' and 'the stream of hopes seemed all running back'. Pip's concern for Magwitch having returned is now firmly based upon his compassion for the dying man, and he is grieved 'to think he had come home for my sake'. The naivety of Magwitch's response is that he believes that Pip can be a 'gentleman without me', as if one can separate one's inheritance from its creator. The idea of coming home also reinforces the connection between Magwitch and Pip which appears in chapter 42 where the convict refers to his own childhood identity as 'I first became aware of myself, down in Essex, a thieving turnips for my living'. The echo here is, of course, of chapter 1 where Pip first has an awareness of the identity of himself as 'the small bundle of shivers growing afraid of it all and beginning to cry . . .'

There is another grim reminder of Wemmick's cultivation of his garden, his 'greenhouse', in the reference made by Magwitch to Pip's visiting him in Newgate 'by chance alonger Wemmick'. The convict recognizes here that Pip might feel tainted by the connection and want to separate himself from his origins. However, Pip has learned the disloyalty of that approach and responds in emphatic terms:

> 'I will never stir from your side . . . when I am suffered to be near you. Please God, I will be as true to you as you have been to me!'

The most striking contrast here is perhaps with the passage from chapter 19 when Pip strolls out alone having heard of his new fortune:

> If I had often thought before, with something allied to shame, of my companionship with the fugitive whom I had once seen limping among those graves, what were my thoughts on this Sunday, when the place recalled the wretch, ragged and shivering, with his felon iron and badge! My comfort was, that it happened a long time ago, and that he had doubtless been transported a long way off, and that he was dead to me, and might be veritably dead into the bargain.

> (p. 147)

The complacent smugness of this approach is contrasted with Magwitch's response to Pip's affirmation that he will stay by his side and be 'as true to you as you have been to me!' when he trembles, turns away his face and makes the clicking sound in his throat of tears being held back. The first time that this action had been noticed was in response to Pip's declaration that he hadn't been a 'deceiving imp' who had brought people with him to arrest the convict on the marshes, and there it is suggestive of self-pity:

> 'You'd be but a fierce young hound indeed, if at your time of life you could help to hunt a wretched warmint, hunted as near death and dunghill as this poor wretched warmint is!'
> Something clicked in his throat as if he had works in him like a clock, and was going to strike. And he smeared his ragged rough sleeve over his eyes.
>
> (p.19)

The second reference to the action comes after Joe makes his compassionate speech concerning the theft of the pie:

> 'God knows you're welcome to it – so far as it was ever mine . . . We don't know what you have done, but we wouldn't have you starved to death for it, poor miserable fellow-creatur – Would us, Pip?'
>
> (p. 40)

This 'click' in the throat, prompted by an awareness of an act of fellow-humanity acts, of course, as a direct contrast to the 'mantrap' set by Jaggers in chapter 24: 'Suddenly – click – you're caught!'

Pip recognizes the odious feeling of self-righteousness expressed by the guests at Mrs Joe's table on Christmas morning. He has recently returned from having fed the convict on 'wittles' and now recognizes the delight with which the assembled company are enlivened by the news of the pursuit of the escaped convicts:

> I thought what terrible good sauce for a dinner my fugitive friend on the marshes was. They had not enjoyed themselves a quarter so much, before the entertainment was brightened with the excitement he furnished.
>
> (p. 33)

Pip rides on Joe's back as a voluntary spectator of the chase in chapter 5 and this is now reversed by Pip steering the boat rowed by his friends down the river to assist Magwitch in his bid for escape from the pursuing law officers. In what seems like a staging post between these two attitudes, in chapter 28 Pip travels down to see Miss Havisham with the convicts on the same coach:

> the convicts hauled themselves up as well as they could, and the convict I had recognised sat behind me with his breath on the hair of my head.

(p. 228)

PASSAGE 10

'Not wishful to intrude. I have departured fur you are well again dear Pip and will do better without.   Jo.'

'P.S. Ever the best of friends.'

Enclosed in the letter was a receipt for the debt and costs on which I had been arrested. Down to that moment I had vainly supposed that my creditor had withdrawn or suspended proceedings until I should be quite recovered. I had never dreamed of Joe's having paid the money; but Joe had paid it, and the receipt was in his name.

What remained for me now, but to follow him to the dear old forge, and there to have out my disclosure to him, and my penitent remonstrance with him, and there to relieve my mind and heart of that reserved Secondly, which had begun as a vague something lingering in my thoughts, and had formed into a settled purpose?

The purpose was, that I would go to Biddy, that I would show her how humbled and repentant I came back, that I would tell her how I had lost all I had once hoped for, that I would remind her of our old confidences in my first unhappy time. Then I would say to her, 'Biddy, I think you once liked me very well, when my errant heart, even while it strayed away from you, was quieter and better with you than it ever has been since. If you can like me only half as well once more, if you can take me with all my faults and disappointments on my head, if you can receive me like a forgiven child (and indeed I am as sorry, Biddy, and have as much need of a hushing voice and a soothing hand), I hope that I am a little worthier of you than I was – not much, but a little. And, Biddy, it shall rest with you to say whether I shall work at the forge with Joe, or whether I shall try for any different occupation down in this country, or whether we shall go away to a distant place where an opportunity awaits me which I set aside when it was offered, until I knew your answer. And now, dear Biddy, if you can tell me that you will go through the world with me, you will surely make it a better world for me, and me a better man for it, and I will try hard to make it a better world for you.'

Such was my purpose. After three days more of recovery, I went down to the old place, to put it in execution. And how I sped in it, is all I have left to tell.

(chapter 57, p. 472)

The 1867 running heads place Joe very firmly at the centre of chapter 57: 'Joe tends me in my sickness/Joe and I talk things over/Things necessary and unnecessary/Joe delicately leaves me'. As Pip falls into the delirium of illness he is arrested for debt, and the officers who arrive seem merged in his delirious state with the attempted escape of Magwitch, the burning of Miss Havisham and the murderous Orlick:

Whether I really had been down in Garden-court in the dead of the night, groping about for the boat that I supposed to be there; whether I had two or three times come to myself on the staircase with great terror, not knowing how I had got out of bed; whether I had found myself lighting the lamp, possessed by the idea that he was coming up the stairs, and that the lights were blown out; whether I had been inexpressibly harassed by the distracted talking, laughing and groaning, of someone, and had half suspected those sounds to be of my own making; whether there had been a closed iron furnace in a dark corner of the room, and a voice had called out over and over again that Miss Havisham was consuming within it; these were things that I tried to settle with myself and get into some order, as I lay that morning on my bed. But the vapour of a limekiln would come between me and them, disordering them all, and it was through the vapour at last that I saw two men looking at me.

(p. 461)

The fears felt by the young Pip at the opening of the novel have returned accompanied by the sense of doing something illicit 'in the dead of night', finding himself on the staircase in 'great terror' and haunted by the threatened return of the convict 'coming up the stairs'. The secret world of inheritance linked with burning hatred and a desire for revenge seems to be contained in the image of the furnace with the vapour of the limekiln where Pip was nearly murdered seeming to usher in the two officers. One of the men bends down to touch Pip on the shoulder to signal his arrest and requests him to 'come to my house'. The house in question is a sponging house in which he confines debtors at their own expense until they can pay. Both the physical gesture and the apparent solicitude are in marked contrast with Joe's arrival to take care of Pip:

> After I had turned the worst point of my illness, I began to notice that while all its other features changed, this one consistent feature did not change. Whoever came about me, still settled down into Joe. I opened my eyes in the night, and I saw in the great chair at the bedside, Joe. I opened my eyes in the day, and, sitting on the window-seat, smoking his pipe in the shaded open window, still I saw Joe. I asked for cooling drink, and the dear hand that gave it me was Joe's. I sank back on my pillow after drinking, and the face that looked so hopefully and tenderly upon me was the face of Joe.
>
> (p. 463)

However, what Pip does not yet fully appreciate is the sensitive intelligence of Joe who has a greater understanding than he does of the impossibility of ever going back into a past that no longer exists.

Pip 'was slow to gain strength' and Joe stays with him, leading him to feel as though he is being looked after like a child: 'I fancied I was little Pip again.' However, as Pip recovers, Joe respectfully retreats into an awareness of class difference that has been caused by the 'great expectations'. This emphasizes the impossibility of ever returning to a relationship which was founded upon innocence before secrecy and lies intruded. The barrier erected between Pip and Joe was first placed there by Pip's inability to share the truth with him concerning the theft at the opening of the novel and the continued existence of this barrier is central to the conversation they now have about the origin of the 'great expectations'. When Pip asks Joe if he wishes to know who the real benefactor was, Joe replies 'why go into subjects, old chap, which as betwixt two sech must be for ever onnecessary?' He then goes on to refer to the world of punishment which Pip was subject to as a child and how he had tried to come between him and the cane, 'tickler'. It is as though the stain of original crime, theft and lies, an association with a felon, still lingers in the mind of both of them and it is this which prompts Pip to decide 'to follow him to the dear old forge, and there to have out my discourse to him, and my penitent remonstrance with him.'

Pip's desire for a simple return to childhood safety is linked to his feelings for Biddy. The reference to the word 'Secondly' takes us back to chapter 55 when Pip hears the language used by Herbert about Clara:

'The dear little thing . . . holds dutifully to her father as long as he lasts . . . I shall come back for the dear little thing, and the dear little thing and I will walk quietly into the nearest church.'

(p. 450)

Interestingly, in passage 10 'that reserved Secondly, which had begun as a vague something lingering in my thoughts' now becomes 'a settled purpose'. However, the language that Pip uses has a patronizing air, and is certainly more evocative of a relationship between mother and son than of that between two lovers who are on the brink of marriage: 'if you can receive me like a forgiven child'. Selfishly, he is capable of contemplating 'whether we shall go away to a distant place where an opportunity awaits me which I set aside when it was offered', and hence of removing Biddy from being Joe's companion. The egotistical and self-pitying aspects of the passage are firmly placed in juxtaposition to the directness of Joe's note which acknowledges that Pip has moved on into a world where he 'will do better without' him. This acknowledgement is accompanied by the enduring love of 'Ever the best of friends', and the simplicity of leaving the receipt 'for the debt and costs on which I had been arrested' without alluding to it in his note.

When Pip does return to the Forge after an absence of eleven years, he looks in through the door to see a domestic scene which is the counterpart of his own childhood. Here, however, love and care have replaced threats and 'tickler':

There, smoking his pipe in the old place by the kitchen firelight, as hale and as strong as ever though a little grey, sat Joe; and there, fenced into the corner with Joe's leg, and sitting on my own little stool looking at the fire, was – I again!

(p. 481)

As if he were in the process of practising a re-run of the novel, Pip asks Biddy if he can borrow the child therefore replacing the figure of Magwitch in relation to the young boy:

> 'Biddy,' said I , when I talked with her after dinner, as her little girl lay sleeping in her lap, 'you must give Pip to me, one of these days; or lend him at all events.'
>
> (p. 481)

While we may well imagine what Mrs Joe's reaction to such an offer might have been, we recognize the difference here when we see the loving reaction from Biddy:

> Biddy looked down at her child, and put its little hand to her lips, and then put the good matronly hand with which she had touched it, into mine.
>
> (p. 481)

As she declines his offer she tells him that he must marry. In a sense he cannot spend the rest of his life looking in on the lives of others and living vicariously.

STUDY QUESTION

1. Choose **one** passage from **each** of the three volumes of *Great Expectations*, and write a close critical analysis of it, trying to bring out how each passage relates to the themes and style of the novel as a whole.

CHAPTER 4

CRITICAL RECEPTION AND PUBLISHING HISTORY

The first weekly instalment of *Great Expectations* appeared in *All the Year Round* on 1 December 1860, and it continued to appear until 3 August 1861. A three-volume edition was published by Chapman and Hall in July 1861. While many of the contemporary reviews of *Great Expectations* were not glowing, the weekly sales of *All the Year Round* rose to about 100,000 copies per week, which led Dickens to publish the novel in three volumes for purchase by lending libraries. In November 1862, a one-volume edition was published containing a revision of the last line of the novel. This change, which became the accepted one for many later editions, will be discussed later on in this chapter when I look at the variant endings to the novel.

A development of critical attitudes towards *Great Expectations* may be linked to a shift in reading habits since its publication, and a growing distrust of what was perceived to be Dickens's popularity with such a wide range of readers. According to J. A. Sutherland, by 1870 *All the Year Round* was selling 300,000 copies per week and reaching half the population of London. In 1870, Forster's Elementary Education Act meant that universal elementary education was introduced in England and Wales for all children between five and thirteen and, according to Janice Carlisle, this had the effect not only of enlarging the number of readers but also of emphasizing the differences between those who were barely literate and the more highly educated readers (see the introduction to the Bedford edition of *Great Expectations*). Carlisle also suggests that 'new printing technologies made possible the publication of serialized fiction in specialized magazines that catered profitably to smaller and more highly differentiated groups of readers than those for whom mid-Victorian novelists had written' (*ibid.*, p. 452). In addition to this, the three-volume novel was superseded by the cheaper format one-volume novel which could be sold directly to the reader rather than the library. All this notwithstanding, in 1882 Mowbray Morris suggested in *Fortnightly Review* that *Great Expectations* was one of Dickens's least popular works and in James Cook's Bibliography of 1879 it is listed as a 'minor work'.

CONTEMPORARY REVIEWS

An unsigned review in *The Times* of 17 October 1861 starts by praising Dickens for his return to the manner of the early writings:

> Mr Dickens has good-naturedly granted to his hosts of readers the desire of their hearts. They have been complaining that in his later works he has adopted a new style, to the neglect of that old manner which first won our admiration. Give us back the old *Pickwick* style, they cried, with its contempt of art, its loose story, its jumbled characters, and all its jesting that made us laugh so lustily; give us back Sam Weller and Mrs Gamp and Bob Sawyer, and Mrs Nickleby, Pecksniff, Bumble, and the rest, and we are willing to sacrifice serious purpose, consistent plot, finished writing, and all else.

The review carried on to note the similarities between *Great Expectations* and *Oliver Twist*:

> The hero of the present tale, Pip, is a sort of Oliver. He is low-born, fatherless and motherless, and he rises out of the cheerless degradation of his childhood into quite another sphere. The thieves get a hold of Oliver, tried to make him a pickpocket, and were succeeded in their friendly intentions by Mr Brownlow, who thought that he could manage better for the lad. Pip's life is not less mixed up with the ways of convicts. He befriends a convict in his need, and henceforth his destiny is involved in that of the prisoner. The convict in the new story takes the place of Mr Brownlow in the old, and supplies Master Pip with every luxury. In either tale, through some unaccountable caprice of fortune, the puny son of poverty suddenly finds himself the child of affluence.
> (from Collins, *Charles Dickens: The Critical Heritage*, p. 430)

The view that Dickens's work had been falling off is most noticeable in the unsigned *Saturday Review* of *The Uncommercial Traveller*, 23 February 1861:

> There is no possibility of pretending that *Bleak House, Little Dorrit*, and *The Two Cities* were not surprisingly bad – melodramatic, pretentious, and, above all, deadly dull. It seemed scarcely conceivable that a writer who had drawn Sam Weller and Mrs Nickleby should really compose the dreary narrative of *Little Dorrit* and her wooden lover.
>
> (from Collins, p. 434)

For some critics there was the yearning for a repetition of the burlesque world of Pickwick and they were left disappointed by what have become the now more recognized and admired qualities which are central to a psychological exploration of guilt: the world of Jungian or Freudian analysis was still many years away. Although G. H. Lewes wrote in 1872 of the hallucinatory qualities in Dickens's writing and the phantasmagoric qualities of Dickens's vision, an unsigned review in the *Dublin University Magazine* of December 1861 makes abundantly clear a sense of disappointment about the new weekly tale:

> . . . how many of those who have helped to carry *Great Expectations* into a fourth or even fifth edition, entered on the reading of it with any serious hope of finding in Pip's adventures a worthy pendant to those of *Pickwick* or *Martin Chuzzlewit*? Would it not be far nearer the truth to say, that nine persons out of ten have approached these volumes with no other feeling than one of kindly regard for the most trivial utterances of an old favourite, or of curiosity, half painful, half careless, to see what further ravages time might have yet in store for the mental frame of a novelist already past his prime?
>
> (from Collins, pp. 408–12)

This hearkening back to the picaresque humour of the early Dickens, with its close relation to the eighteenth century of Fielding and Smollett, found an outlet in the *Rambler* review of January 1862:

Yet, with all his faults, we should be puzzled to name Mr Dickens's equal in the perception of the purely farcical, ludicrous, and preposterously funny, though not so much now, perhaps, as in the days when he had not adopted the stage-trick of putting some queer saying into his characters' mouths, and making them utter it on every possible occasion. It is by a partial flickering up of this bright gift that *Great Expectations* has proved an agreeable surprise to so many of his readers. The story is as exaggerated and impossible as any he ever perpetrated; it is uncomfortable, too, and abounds with those tedious repetitions to which he has become so grievously addicted. Mr Jaggers is always biting his forefinger; Provis begins his speeches with a stereotyped phrase. But there is some very good fun in the story, nevertheless; not jovial, not hearty, not Pickwickian indeed, but really comic, and sufficient to excite a pleasant quiet laugh on a dull winter-day.

(from Collins, pp. 434–6)

Mrs Oliphant's article on 'Sensation Novels' for *Blackwood's Edinburgh Magazine* in May 1862 also highlighted the sense that Dickens's writing has lost its power:

One feels that he must have got tired of it as the work went on, and that the creatures he had called into being, but who are no longer the lively men and women they used to be, must have bored him unspeakably before it was time to cut short their career, and throw a hasty and impatient hint of their future to stop the tiresome public appetite.

To Mrs Oliphant's mind, Joe Gargery is the only character who continues the much-loved mood of the author: 'He is as good, as true, patient, and affectionate, as ungrammatical and confused in his faculty of speech, as could be desired', and he possesses 'all that affecting tenderness and refinement of affection with which Mr Dickens has the faculty of making his poor blacksmiths and fishermen much more interesting than anything he has ever produced in the condition of gentleman.'

Mrs Oliphant sees the introduction of Miss Havisham as 'fancy run mad' and is unconvinced of her reality, wondering about the wedding-dress which in the quarter of a century 'had only grown yellow and faded, but was still, it appears, extant in all its integrity, no tatters being so much as inferred . . .' She is more convinced by 'the darker side of the story':

> The appearance of the escaped convict in the squalid and dismal solitude of the marsh – the melancholy landscape with that one wretched figure embodying the forlorn and desolate sentiment of the scene – is perhaps as vivid and effective a sketch as Mr Dickens ever drew. It is made in fewer words than usual, done at a breath, as if the author felt what he was saying this time, and saw the scene too vividly himself to think a full development of every detail necessary to enable his reader to see it also.
>
> After another very vivid picture of the same marshes under the wild torchlight of a convict-hunt, this horrible figure disappears out of the book, and only comes to life again at the end of the second volume, when, as Pip's unknown benefactor, the mysterious secret friend who has made the young blacksmith a gentleman, he re-emerges, humanised and horribly affectionate, out of the darkness. The young fellow's utter despair when he finds himself held fast in the clutches of this man's gratitude and bounty – compelled to be grateful in his turn while loathing the very thought of the obligation which he has been unwittingly incurring – is very powerfully drawn, and the predicament perhaps as strange and frightful as could be conceived . . .

While the unreality of the story seems to have been an object of focus in some early criticism of the novel, Edwin P. Whipple's review in *Atlantic Monthly*, September 1861, provides a different perspective:

> The plot of *Great Expectations* is also noticeable as indicating, better than any of his previous stories, the individuality of Dickens's genius. Everybody must have discerned in the action of his mind two diverging tendencies, which, in this novel, are harmonized. He possesses a singularly wide, clear, and minute power of accurate observation, both of things and of persons; but his observation, keen and true to actualities as it independently is, is not a dominant faculty, and is opposed or controlled by the strong tendency of his disposition to pathetic or humorous idealization.
>
> In *Great Expectations* . . . the general impression is not one of objective reality. The author palpably uses his observations as

materials for his creative faculties to work upon; he does not record, but invents; and he produces something which is natural only under conditions prescribed by his own mind. He shapes, disposes, penetrates, colours, and contrives everything, and the whole action is a series of events which could have occurred only in his own brain, and which it is difficult to conceive of as actually 'happening'. And yet in none of his other works does he evince a shrewder insight into real life, and a clearer perception and knowledge of what is called 'the world'.

The autobiographical form of the novel may have prompted the *Saturday Review* to comment that in *Great Expectations* there is a 'more profound study of the general nature of human character than Dickens usually betrays' and that 'the hero writes an autobiography of his own life, tells the story of his childhood'. This perception of the novel as a *bildungsroman* has dominated critical attitude since then and many critics have concentrated either upon the contrast between a growing boy and the society which surrounds him or the psychological development of a maimed child. Extracts from three early twentieth-century reactions to the novel are included below (quoted from Wall, pp. 244, 253).

1. G. K. Chesterton: 'When he sets out to describe Pip's great expectation he does not set out, as in a fairy tale, with the idea that these great expectations will be fulfilled; he sets out from the first with the idea that these great expectations will be disappointing.' 1906.
2. A. C. Swinburne: '. . . of all first chapters is there any comparable for impression and for fusion of humour and terror and pity and fancy and truth to that which confronts the child with the convict on the marshes in the twilight? . . . The ghastly tragedy of Miss Havisham could only have been made at once credible and endurable by Dickens; he alone could have reconciled the strange and sordid horror with the noble and pathetic survival of possible emotion and repentance.' 1913.
3. Ernest A. Baker: 'It is Dickens's one serious study of the growth of personality; and, though he lets Pip tell the story, he manages with great skill to bring out the true significance and the humour of the strange situations, without showing his own hand, and, notably, without the heavy moralizing which Thackeray put

in the mouth of his imaginary autobiographer in *Lovel the Widower*, which appeared in the same year.' 1957.

In reference to this last comment, Thackeray's novel appeared in the *Cornhill Magazine*, and contains references to a youthful love attachment which is presented in a decidedly more humorous and lighter vein than in *Great Expectations*. The narrator contemplates having his photograph taken, and wonders 'Would Some One (I have said, I think, that the party in question is well married in a distant island) like to have the thing, I wonder, and be reminded of a man whom she knew in life's prime, with brown curly locks, as she looked on the effigy of this elderly gentleman, with a forehead as bare as a billiard-ball?' In his privately printed *Some Notes on the Outlook and Procedures of the Post-Romantic Mind*, November 1968, J. H. Prynne referred to Thackeray's reactions in his 'Roundabout Papers, No. 8' (1860) to Pierce Egan's *Life in London*, in which three picaresque men-about-town make a visit to the condemned yard of Newgate Prison:

> Thackeray, describing his reactions in 1860 to re-reading this passage, comments on the excellence of the plate by the brothers Cruikshank illustrating the Newgate scene, only to continue: 'Now we haste away to merrier scenes: to Tattersall's (ah! Gracious powers! What a funny fellow that actor was who performed Dicky Green in that scene at the play!); and now we are at a private party . . .' This sporting and jolly attitude to scenes from town life makes *Pickwick Papers* entirely understandable as part of the nostalgic genre, and makes the portrait of the Marshalsea Prison in *Little Dorrit* (1855–57) only the more astonishingly powerful and unprepared-for.

By emphasizing Thackeray's reactions Prynne draws attention to the tendency of the reading public to prefer to distance themselves from the uncomfortable picture of pervading imprisonment which is presented by Dickens.

MORE RECENT CRITICAL ANALYSIS

Edmund Wilson's essay, 'Dickens: the Two Scrooges', (1941) was central in pointing out the psychological aspects of characters who are torn between their public persona and their submerged selves which are continually jostling to assert their own validity. This idea of their being more than one 'self' was taken up by Dorothy Van Ghent (1953) who highlighted the similarities between Miss Havisham and Estella, Pip and Magwitch and Joe and Orlick. Julian Moynahan's development of this critical stance is outlined below in greater detail. Sociological criticism concentrated more on the relationship between the protagonist and the society around him by whose standards he is both encouraged and condemned. The undertow of material prosperity was recognised by Lionel Trilling to consist of 'hulks', murder, rats and 'decay in the cellarage of the novel':

> The greatness of *Great Expectations* begins in its title: modern society bases itself on great expectations which, if ever they are realized, are found to exist by reason of a sordid, hidden reality.

In the second half of the twentieth century, criticism of the novel has been dominated by concentration on the psychological development of Pip as a guilt-ridden hero. Three particularly influential approaches are outlined below:

1. *CHARLES DICKENS: THE WORLD OF HIS NOVELS*, J. HILLIS MILLER 1958

Great Expectations is the most unified and concentrated expression of Dickens' abiding sense of the world, and Pip might be called the archetypal Dickens hero. In *Great Expectations* Dickens' particular view of things is expressed with a concreteness and symbolic intensity he never surpassed.

(Hillis Miller, p. 249)

This unified sense may be interestingly linked to the restrictions of weekly publication and a shorter length of novel both leading to an increase in intensity and complexity. Hillis Miller highlights the novel's opening which, 'like most of Dickens' novels, does not begin with a description of the perfect bliss of childhood, the period when the world and the self are identified, and the parents are seen as benign gods whose care and whose overlooking judgement protect and justify the child.' He emphasizes the position of the child who 'becomes aware of himself as isolated from all that is outside of himself. The Dickensian hero is separated from nature.' In addition, the child is often an orphan or is illegitimate:

> He has no status in the community, no inherited role which he can accept with dignity. He is characterized by desire, rather than by possession. His spiritual state is one of an expectation founded on a present consciousness of lack, of deprivation.
>
> (*ibid.*, p. 251)

This sense of absence is also accompanied by a feeling of guilt where 'His very existence is a matter of reproach and a shameful thing', and is accompanied by a desire to reverse the circumstances in which he finds himself:

> In a world where the only possible relation to other people seems to be that of oppressor to oppressed, or oppressed to oppressor, those who are born into oppression may try to seize the role of oppressor.
>
> (*ibid.*)

This struggle for power can be seen on one level with Wemmick, 'himself a victim of the great legal organization', who takes control of the plants in his flower-garden of Newgate or with Magwitch who turns Pip upside down 'as though to reverse their roles'. However, two more surreptitious ways of domination are highlighted in both Magwitch and Miss Havisham who manipulate others 'as the agent of his revenge on society: In one way or another several characters in *Great Expectations* try to *make* other characters':

> At the centre of Dickens' novels is a recognition of the bankruptcy of the relation of the individual to society as it now exists, the objective structure of given institutions and values. Only what an individual makes of himself, in charitable relations to others, counts. And this self-creation tends to require open revolt against the pressures of society. Human beings are themselves the source of the transcendence of their isolation.
>
> (*ibid.*, p. 254)

One of the most interesting criticisms which has developed some of these thoughts is Eiichi Hara's 'Stories Present and Absent in *Great Expectations*' (*English Literary History* 53, 1986):

> If one takes the enigma of Pip's secret benefactor to be the central axis of the novel, as it indeed is, it is clear that the author of the story is not Pip but Magwitch, who has been devising, plotting and writing Pip's story. Magwitch is a character representing the double meaning of 'author': the writer and the father. He is both the author of Pip's story and the father who has secretly adopted him as his son, begetter of the text and its hero at the same time.

2. 'THE HERO'S GUILT: THE CASE OF *GREAT EXPECTATIONS*', JULIAN MOYNAHAN 1960

Pip has certainly one of the guiltiest consciences in literature. He not only suffers *agenbite of inwit* for his sin of snobbish ingratitude toward Joe and Biddy, but also suffers through much of the novel from what can only be called a conviction of criminal guilt. Whereas he expiates his sins of snobbery and ingratitude by ultimately accepting the convict Magwitch's unspoken claim for his protection and help, by willingly renouncing his great expectations, and by returning in a chastened mood to Joe and Biddy, he cannot expiate – or exorcise – his conviction of criminality, because it does not seem to correspond with any real criminal acts or intentions.

I would suggest that Orlick rather than Magwitch is the figure from the criminal milieu of the novel whose relations to him come to define Pip's implicit participation in the acts of violence with which the novel abounds.

Moynahan's essay interestingly points to the parallels between the careers of Pip and Orlick:

- Orlick works side by side with Pip in the Forge.
- While Orlick strikes the blow against Mrs Joe, Pip feels that he supplied the assault weapon.
- Pip is employed by Miss Havisham inside Satis House, but Orlick is employed as the gatekeeper.

- Pip joins up with Magwitch and Orlick with Compeyson.
- Pip's hopes move from the Forge to Satis House to London and Orlick moves his base of operations from the Forge to Satis House to London.
- Pip's tender feelings for Biddy are 'given a distorted echo by Orlick's obviously lecherous interest in the same girl'.

Referring to the nightmare quality of the meeting between the two at the limekiln hut, Moynahan suggests that 'the innocent figure is made the accused and the guilty one the accuser. As in a dream the situation is absurd, yet like a dream it may contain hidden truth . . . Orlick confronts the hero in this scene, not merely as would-be murderer, but also as a distorted and darkened mirror-image'. The psychological background to these sado-masochistic studies in the complex nature of relationships of power between people links Moynahan's essay with the ground-breaking work of Edmund Wilson.

3. 'HOW WE MUST READ GREAT EXPECTATIONS', DICKENS THE NOVELIST, Q. D. LEAVIS 1970

One of the principle reasons for the homogeneous tone of the novel is that it is told us by a narrator who is firmly kept before us as remote from the self who is the subject, a self that is seen in growth from childhood to adult status. Unlike *David Copperfield* the narrator Pip is not identified in sympathy with that child, boy or youth; far from it, the wry glance he directs at his follies and shortcomings and mistakes warns us off any easy sympathy with the youthful Pip.

(Leavis and Leavis, p. 290)

Pip's initial sense of guilt was inevitable, the result of the Victorian theory of the relation between parent and child: Mrs. Joe is supported in her demand for gratitude from Pip by public opinion . . . Even if he had never met the convict the guilt would have been there which made him harbour the suppressed wish to be rid of his sister, and therefore feel himself a candidate for the wicked Noah's Ark on the horizon to which society banished those who broke the law.

(*ibid.*, p. 293)

Dickens had clearly given a great deal of thought to the problem of convincingly freeing Pip from the bonds of selfishness, shame and guilt.

(ibid., p. 324)

Some of the argument put forward by Q. D. Leavis suggests that Pip's aspirations, his desire for 'great expectations', are entirely understandable as an aspect of the Victorian belief in social advancement. She provides a comment about the vividness of the early pages, which is in stark relief to the psychological analyses of Moynahan, when she refers to Pip's sufferings being 'minimised by the amusement with which the adult Pip recounts his memories'. She also adds that 'there is sufficient poignancy in the recollections to make them moving as well as vivid' *(ibid.*, p. 290).

As a measure of the amount of critical attention which has been received by *Great Expectations*, in 1986 George J. Worth published an annotated bibliography of the novel which he divided into three periods – 1870–1939, 1940–1969, 1970–1983. Since then there has been a large number of publications among which the most interesting are Jeremy Tambling's 'Prison-Bound: Dickens, Foucault and *Great Expectations*', Hilary Schor's 'Violence, Desire, and the Woman's Story in *Great Expectations*' and Professor David Trotter's introduction to the 2003 Penguin edition of the novel. Publication details of these and many others will be found in Chapter 6.

THE DIFFERENT ENDINGS OF THE NOVEL

In a letter of 23 June 1861 to Wilkie Collins, Dickens refers to the ending of *Great Expectations* as it was to appear in *All the Year Round*: 'Bulwer was so very anxious that I should alter the end of *Great Expectations* – the extreme end, I mean, after Biddy and Joe are done with – and stated his reasons so well, that I have resumed the wheel, and taken another turn upon it. Upon the whole I think it is for the better. You shall see the change when we meet' (*Letters: Volume 9*, p. 428). Writing to Bulwer Lytton the next day, he enclosed 'the whole of the concluding No. of *Great Expectations*, in order that you may the more readily understand where I have made the change' (*ibid.*). In the same letter Dickens expressed a concern that he may have laboured the rewritten section and got it 'out of proportion'. The revised ending is about 1,000 words long, as opposed to the 300 originally intended. However, in writing to Forster on 1 July he expressed no doubt about the effect of the changes made:

> You will be surprised to hear that I have changed the end of *Great Expectations* from and after Pip's return to Joe's, and finding his little likeness there. Bulwer, who has been, as I think you know, extraordinarily taken by the book, so strongly urged it upon me, after reading the proofs, and supported his views with such good reasons, that I resolved to make the change. I have put in as pretty a little piece of writing as I could, and I have no doubt the story will be more acceptable through the alteration.
>
> (*ibid.*, p. 432)

The original shorter version survives in proof, and it was published in Forster's *Life*. Dickens originally intended the novel to end with chapter 58, when Pip returns to the Forge after an absence of eight years. In his conversation with Biddy he is asked whether he has 'quite forgotten' Estella, and replies:

> 'My dear Biddy, I have forgotten nothing in my life that ever had a foremost place there. But that poor dream, as I once used to call it, has all gone by, Biddy, all gone by!'
>
> It was two years more, before I saw herself. I had heard of her as leading a most unhappy life, and as being separated from her husband who had used her with great cruelty, and who had become quite renowned as a compound of pride, brutality, and meanness. I had heard of the death of her husband (from an accident consequent on ill-treating a horse), and of her being married again to a Shropshire doctor, who, against his interest, had once very manfully interposed, on an occasion when he was in professional attendance on Mr. Drummle, and had witnessed some outrageous treatment of her. I had heard that the Shropshire doctor was not rich, and that they lived on her own personal fortune.
>
> I was in England again – in London, and walking along Piccadilly with little Pip – when a servant came running after me to ask would I step back to a lady in a carriage who wished to speak to me. It was a little pony carriage, which the lady was driving; and the lady and I looked sadly enough on one another.

'I am greatly changed, I know; but I thought you would like to shake hands with Estella too, Pip. Lift up that pretty child and let me kiss it!' (She supposed the child, I think, to be my child.)

I was very glad afterwards to have had the interview; for, in her face and in her voice, and in her touch, she gave me the assurance, that suffering had been stronger than Miss Havisham's teaching, and had given her a heart to understand what my heart used to be.

The revised ending continues from Pip's visit to the Forge having spent eleven rather than eight years in the East, and it involves 'a walk over to the old spot before dark'. When he arrives at Satis House, 'the day had quite declined':

There was no house now, no brewery, no building whatever left, but the wall of the old garden. The cleared space had been enclosed with a rough fence, and, looking over it, I saw that some of the old ivy had struck root anew, and was growing green on low quiet mounds of ruin. A gate in the fence standing ajar, I pushed it open, and went in.

A cold shivery mist had veiled the afternoon, and the moon was not yet up to scatter it. But, the stars were shining beyond the mist, and the moon was coming, and the evening was not dark. I could trace out where every part of the old house had been, and where the brewery had been, and where the gates, and where the casks. I had done so, and was looking along the desolate garden-walk, when I beheld a solitary figure in it.

The figure showed itself aware of me, as I advanced. It had been moving towards me, but it stood still. As I drew nearer, I saw it to be the figure of a woman. As I drew nearer yet, it was about to turn away, when it stopped, and let me come up with it. Then, it faltered as if much surprised, and uttered my name, and I cried out:

'Estella!'

(p. 482)

During the conversation between Pip and Estella it transpires that the ground they are on belongs to Estella now, 'the only possession I have not relinquished', and she intends to build upon it. The reason for her visit, the first one since the fire, is so that she can 'take leave of it before its change'. The forward-looking qualities of the tone of this writing echo the reference to the green ivy growing over the ruins. The stars, associated with Estella's name, are shining and the clarity of Pip's memory is emphasized by his ability to 'trace out where every part of the old house had been'. A measure of the ambiguity attached to this rewritten ending is felt by the reader as we are informed that 'The freshness of her beauty was indeed gone', and we recall the earlier references to her disastrous marriage to Bentley Drummle, concluding in his death:

> This release had befallen her some two years before; for anything I knew, she was married again.

As they prepare to separate, as friends, Estella suggests that they will 'continue friends apart'. Her last words are, however, contradicted to some extent by the concluding paragraph:

> I took her hand in mine, and we went out of the ruined place; and, as the morning mists had risen long ago when I first left the forge, so, the evening mists were rising now, and in all the broad expanse of tranquil light they showed to me, I saw the shadow of no parting from her.

The implication that they are now to remain together is heightened by the reference here to the closing of Book XII of Milton's *Paradise Lost*, where 'evening mist' glides over the marshes and 'gathers ground fast at the labourer's heel/Homeward returning'. The last line had itself been subject to change since the manuscript reads 'I saw the shadow of no parting from her but one' which Dickens altered at proof stage by removing the last two words. The inference behind the two words may be that the final parting will be that of death. The paragraph quoted above remained the one published in *All the Year Round* and in the 1861 three-volume edition. However, for the 1862 one-volume edition, the line was subject to further revision so that it became 'I saw no shadow of another parting from her' and that is how it remained for the 1867 Charles Dickens edition of his works.

Perhaps the most comprehensive discussion of the relative merits of the different endings can be found in Edgar Rosenberg's 'Last

Words on *Great Expectations*: A Textual Brief on the Six Endings', which was published in the *Dickens Studies Annual* 9 (1981).

STUDY QUESTIONS

1. Lionel Trilling's comments on *Great Expectations* suggested that its 'greatness' began in its title: 'modern society bases itself on great expectations which, if ever they are realized, are found to exist by reason of a sordid, hidden reality.' How true do you find this comment in the light of other novels which you have read? In nineteenth-century fiction you might look at George Eliot's *Middlemarch*. As an interesting reflection on this idea you might also look at Graham Swift's novel of the 1980s, *Waterland*.
2. Having studied the variant endings of the novel, decide which you prefer and give clear reasons for your choice. How much of your decision is based upon your own desire as a reader for a particular ending and how much is based upon what you feel is appropriate for the novel itself?
3. To some critics, *Great Expectations* is a realistic account of life in the first decades of the nineteenth century, while to others it portrays a world which is both fantastic and grotesque. Is it possible to argue the case from both points of view?

CHAPTER 5

ADAPTATION, INTERPRETATION AND INFLUENCE

The weekly publication of *Great Expectations* in *All the Year Round* was not illustrated, and neither was the first edition. Since this was the first and only one of Dickens's novels in which there was not a collaboration between the author and a graphic artist, there has been some considerable speculation as to what may have happened. Hablôt K. Browne (Phiz), who had illustrated most of the novels from *Pickwick* to *Little Dorrit* and *A Tale of Two Cities*, was not approached to do illustrations for *Great Expectations* when invitations for illustrating the Library Edition were being issued for publication in 1864. The commission for eight woodcuts to accompany the text was given to Marcus Stone, who then went on to illustrate *Our Mutual Friend* which was published in 20 monthly parts. A suggestion that Dickens and Browne may have fallen out rests partly on a letter sent by the illustrator to Robert Young:

> Marcus is no doubt to do Dickens. I have been a 'good boy', I believe. The plates in hand are all in good time, so that I do not know what's 'up', any more than you. Dickens probably thinks a new hand would give his old puppets a fresh look, or perhaps he does not like my illustrating Trollope neck-and-neck with him – though, by Jingo, he need fear no rivalry *there*! Confound all authors and publishers, say I. There is no pleasing one or t'other. I wish I had never had anything to do with the lot.
>
> (Lester, p. 180)

However, as John Harvey points out, in his seminal work *Victorian Novelists and their Illustrators*, the root causes of the collapse of the relationship between Browne and Dickens go back before *Great Expectations*. He points out that 'Traces of discontent show in the transactions relating to *Little Dorrit*, and it is significant that none of the illustrations to that work and *A Tale of Two Cities* bear Browne's signature, and that Browne burned his correspondence with authors' (Harvey, p. 164).

The interest which Dickens took in the work of young Marcus Stone, the son of Frank Stone the artist who had died in November 1859, is evidenced in the letters written to publishers. In November 1859 Dickens wrote to Thomas Longman:

> I am very anxious to present to you, with the earnest hope that you will hold him in your remembrance, young Mr. Marcus Stone, son of poor Frank Stone who died suddenly, but a little week ago.
>
> You know, I dare say, what a start this young man made in the last Exhibition, and what a favourable notice his picture attracted. He wishes to make an additional opening for himself in the illustration of books. He is an admirable draughtsman – has a most dextrous hand – a charming sense of grace and beauty – and a capital power of observation.
>
> (*Letters: Volume 9*, p. 170)

The Royal Academy picture which Dickens referred to was titled 'Silent Pleading' and presented an old wanderer saved by a stranger. He also sent introductory letters to Chapman and Hall and to John Murray. The letter of introduction to Chapman and Hall was taken up when the firm asked Stone to illustrate the one-volume edition of *Great Expectations* in 1862 and the Illustrated Library edition of 1864. Perhaps the clearest sign of discord between Dickens and Browne was the decision to use the new illustrator to do the work for the Illustrated Library edition of *Tale of Two Cities* rather than simply reproducing Browne's own original drawings.

In her essay, 'The Dickens Illustrations: Their Function', Mrs Leavis raises the question of whether we can imagine satisfactory illustrations to this novel and suggests that whereas Browne might have 'done well enough by the few residues of satire such as the Pocket household, Barnard's Inn and the Wemmick-Jaggers office with its squalid clients' it would have taken a variety of illustrators to realize the novel's 'complexity, range and unique greatness' (Leavis and Leavis, p. 362). However, the importance of the satire which is central to Hogarthian moral vision, the contrast between 'The Idle and Industrious Apprentice', is emphasized by Wopsle's reading in chapter 15 of Lillo's *The London Merchant, or, The History of George Barnwell*. Lillo's domestic tragedy, first performed in 1731, features a young apprentice who is seduced by the beauty of Sarah Millwood and led into the robbing of his master and the murder of his uncle. Both Barnwell and his lady accomplice end up on the gallows at Newgate. When he entertains both Pumblechook and Pip to his lengthy dramatization of the tale, Wopsle 'took pains to present me in the worst light':

> At once ferocious and maudlin, I was made to murder my uncle with no extenuation circumstances whatever; Millwood put me down in argument, on every occasion; it became sheer monomania in my master's daughter to care a button for me.

As Barnwell is hanged at Newgate, Pip recognizes that 'all I can say for my gasping and procrastinating conduct on the fatal morning, is, that it was worthy of the general feebleness of my character' (chapter 15). Pumblechook shakes his head at Pip as he advises him to 'take warning' as if he already associated him with the criminal who 'contemplated murdering a near relation.'

'The Harlot's Progress', which Hogarth produced in 1732, centred on the corruption of a young girl who moved from the country to the town, took up life as a prostitute and declined into an early death. This was followed in 1733 by a sequel, 'The Rake's Progress', which mirrored the action of the former by illustrating a young man's decline into crime, drunkenness and insanity. The idea of a 'Progress' was adopted by George Cruikshank in his series of illustrations 'The Bottle' and was used as a subtitle for Dickens's early Newgate novel, *Oliver Twist, or, The Parish Boy's Progress*. As an example of a *bildungsroman*, *Great Expectations* preserves a connection with these moral pictures from earlier years by having its separate parts divided into 'stages', and by dealing with the country boy who goes to London. The psychological realism of Pip's progress is, however, beyond the moral pattern outlined by Hogarth's prints. There may well be an interesting comparison between some aspects of the novel and Hogarth's plates for Industry and Idleness 1747 as suggested in Paul B. Davis's article, 'Dickens, Hogarth, and the Illustrated *Great Expectations*', but they relate to the aspects of the novel which fit into the genre of Newgate fiction rather than those which contemplate the subtle interrelationship of character and event which go to form the growing Pip. The idea of 'progress' and social climbing is, of course, common to the works of both artists:

> Dickens's most self-conscious presentation of social climbing, *Great Expectations* extends the contrasts between the idle and industrious apprentices. In earlier novels Frank Goodchild reappears as Walter Gay, David Copperfield, and Charles Darnay, while Idle surfaces as Uriah Heep, Richard Carstone, and Sydney Carton. Pip combines the two figures. As the young-man-come-to-London destined to marry Estella, he plays a Whittington-role, while he acts an idle Jack Sheppard in his guilty resentment at the forge and his dissipation with the Finches of the Grove.

In Plate 5 of Hogarth's series, 'The Idle 'Prentice turn'd away and sent to Sea', the gallows, with a man hanging from it, looms on the horizon as a warning to the young apprentice in a manner which reminds us of the 'gibbet, with some chains hanging to it which once held a pirate', an image which dominates the last paragraph of chapter 1 of *Great Expectations*. However, whereas the Hogarth print offers a static symbolic presence, the description in Dickens has a fluidity of movement which is nightmarish:

> On the edge of the river I could faintly make out the only two black things in all the prospect that seemed to be standing upright; one of these was the beacon by which sailors steered – like an unhooped cask upon a pole – an ugly thing when you were near it; the other, a gibbet with some chains hanging to it which had once held a pirate.
>
> (p. 7)

The contrast between the path of industry, lighted by the beacon, and the path of idleness, the gallows, is clear but what follows in the prose is phantasmagoric in its movement, reflecting not only a child's nightmarish fears but a disturbing sense that what has appeared once may have the possibility of unhooking itself again:

The man was limping on towards this latter, as if he were the pirate come to life, and come down, and going back to hook himself up again. It gave me a terrible turn when I thought so . . .

(p. 7)

The visual impact of the prose is brought about by the distorted confusions which reflect Pip's state of mind and the best illustrated version of that is probably the opening of David Lean's 1947 film where the landscape has a living quality. The eerie movement of the trees and the bleak distance of the horizon there provide a background out of which the criminal Magwitch can appear like a figure risen from the graves. At the opening of the film, Pip is seen running along a bleak horizon which is dominated by the silhouettes of two gallows placed on it. He runs beneath the second one, hesitating for a second to glance up at it, before entering the churchyard. The bleakness of the skyline and the vividness of the gallows overshadow the landscape: they offer an intimate connection both with the boy himself and the atmosphere which is created by the creaking noise of the trees. One of the large trunks surrounding the churchyard seems to represent a face which would not be out of place in a painting by Arcimboldo, and as Pip is placing his bunch of flowers on the grave of his parents we see a tombstone behind him which has the distinct shape of a head and shoulders. Marcus Stone did not do a woodcut of this opening scene, and judging from the set-piece stasis of his eight illustrations it may have not been within his grasp. By contrast, when F. W. Pailthorpe illustrated the novel in 1885 he caught the tone of the prose rather effectively. As Davis points out:

Pailthorpe's pictures seek to recapture the qualities of the caricatures of Cruikshank and Phiz. Their borders are not 'framed' as on the realistic illustrations of the later nineteenth century. Instead they melt into the page, blurring the distinction between text and picture.

The first plate which John McLenan did for the American serialization of the novel, appearing in the periodical *Harper's Weekly*, captures some of the same atmosphere. It has the title 'The Gibbet on the Marshes', and the watery foreground merges into the heading 'CHAPTER 1'. In Pailthorpe's 'The Terrible Stranger in the Churchyard', the figure of the convict is giant-like as it appears from behind a tombstone with the word 'SACRED'. With one hand out-stretched it appears to lay hold on the terrified boy who has raised his right arm partly to ward off the figure and partly as if to wish to place it in front of his eyes, blocking out the apparition. The power of this illustrative connection between Pip and Magwitch is further emphasized in the later illustration, 'On the Stairs', where the figure from the past, from the other side of the world, has its foot on the stair with both arms outstretched: a figure from the mind's cellarage coming to claim its own. The light in Pip's hand seems almost to beam the intruding figure up, past the door with SHARP written on it, as though he has stared into the abyss and conjured up the true benefactor from whom he can never separate himself.

This inescapable quality of Magwitch is caught disturbingly in the illustrations done by Harry Furniss for the 1910 edition of the novel. In 'Provis', the figure of Magwitch stares out at Pip and at us. He has hands firmly placed on his knees and the stolid look of determination caught in the down-turned mouth gives him the impression of having taken root. The drawing is unsettling precisely because it involves the reader and therefore brings into question the notion of complicity: where do *our* 'great expectations' come from? A similar brooding quality haunts Charles Green's 1877 illustration of Magwitch sitting in Pip's chambers done for the Gadshill Edition. Here Magwitch lours at the fire as though bent upon his own purposes of revenge upon society while Pip pours rum-and-water for him in the background. The intensity of Green's convict marginalizes Pip who is clearly a mere pawn in the older man's purposes of revenge.

The Household Edition of Dickens's novels appeared between 1871 and 1879, and the illustrations for *Great Expectations* were done by F. A. Fraser. John Harvey's comments upon the Household Edition are worth bearing in mind here:

> The draughtsmanship is often sensitive, and the use of light and dark is frequently dramatic, but there is no attempt to communicate any meaning that cannot be expressed by a naturalistic study of character and setting.
>
> (Harvey, p. 162)

The accuracy of this comment can be seen immediately on compar-ing Fraser's first illustration, the appearance of Magwitch in the graveyard, with the Pailthorpe. The impression given is of a tramp who, with his hands on his knees as he bends down to the little boy in front of him, is about to ask him for some money. What is lost is the dramatic quality of nightmare that weaves its way through the text:

> 'Hold your noise!' cried a terrible voice, as a man started up from among the graves at the side of the church porch. 'Keep still, you little devil, or I'll cut your throat!'
>
> (p. 3)

Fraser's Magwitch has lost that sense of surprise and horror, and replaced it with a more pedestrian picture which could adequately reflect a scene from Henry Mayhew's *London Labour and London Poor*. For a return to the phantasmagoric qualities reflected in Dickens's writing one must turn to the illustrations done by Charles Keeping for The Folio Society in 1981. Here the figure of the convict is terrifying as it 'started' from behind a gravestone. The face is manic and the right arm clutches the lower part of Pip's face in a grip which is almost tangible. The overwhelming sense of fear in the scene is further explored by having Magwitch's left hand clutching the top of the gravestone as if blocking out any chance of escape. Keeping's slashed lines and eerie merging of vegetation and human arteries add to the deeply uncomfortable nature of this shocking experience.

Paul Davis feels that, on the whole, Harry Furniss is probably the most successful illustrator of the novel:

> His pictures combine elements from the tradition of caricature with the subjectivity of impressionist technique. Like many modern illustrators, Furniss provides character sketches, but the subjective rendering in his portraits tells as much about Pip as about the character depicted . . . . Furniss's illustration of Pip and Estella in the garden, a subject usually rendered with bland conventional sentimentality, captures Pip's degradation and Estella's arrogance by combining impressionist subjectivity with the dramatic conventions of caricature.

In chapter 29 of the text, Pip and Estella walk round the garden which 'was too overgrown and rank for walking in with ease' and Pip shows her 'to a nicety' where he had seen her walking on the brewery casks 'that first old day'. Estella fails to remember any of the details, including making Pip cry, and he records that 'her not remembering and not minding in the least, made me cry again, inwardly – and that is the sharpest crying of all.' Estella condescends to Pip 'as a brilliant and beautiful woman might' and assures him that she has no heart, 'no softness there, no – sympathy – sentiment – nonsense.' She casts him in the role of her servant: 'you shall be my Page, and give me your shoulder' and they walk round the ruined garden which 'was all in bloom for me'. The trappings of medieval romance hinted at in the text lead to the recognition by Pip that 'Estella looked more bright and beautiful than before, and I was under stronger enchantment.' Furniss's illustration has captured the charm and movement of the scene as Estella leans back arrogantly while she disdainfully touches the shoulder of the young man, whose head is turned downwards. Pip seems to toy with his hat with a touch that reminds us of Joe's difficulties with that article of gentlemanly attire in chapter 27 when he visits Pip in London. Joe's hat is held carefully 'with both hands, like a bird's-nest with eggs in it', and likewise here Pip holds the precious article as though it contains the fragile expectations of gentlemanly advancement. As Davis points out, 'the riotous garden in the background projects Pip's inner turmoil.'

Marcus Stone's last engraving for the novel is titled 'With Estella after all' and it is one of the more successful of his plates. The figure of Pip is that of a mature man, bearded and with down-turned head as if to suggest the weight of the eleven years of absence undergone by him before this last visit home. The stars in the background present the distant quality inherent in Estella's name, but as she leans in towards him and places her left hand gently, as if for support, on his arm there is a clear inference that she is relying upon his strength. The illustration is a reflection of the printed ending of the novel as it was some ten years before Forster's *Life of Dickens* was published with its information concerning the author's original intention for how the novel should end.

In contrast to Stone's solemn feeling of togetherness ('I saw no shadow of another parting from her'), Fraser's last engraving has the subtitle 'We sat down on a bench that was near' and Estella's head looks down with a sense of disappointment and isolation. Pip sits next to her, erect and enquiring, while the broken parapet of wall behind and the thistle growing in the right-hand corner of the plate suggest a scene which might have interestingly illustrated Henry James's late story, 'The Bench of Desolation'. Harry Furniss's last illustration, 'Estella and Pip', takes the reader away from Satis House and presents Pip and Estella in the churchyard. This could be said to have a neatness of structure to it as a parallel to the opening scene of the novel, but it also dictates to us the way we read the future. Furniss presents us with two figures whose future happiness is clearly questioned by the way their heads are both looking forward but with no interchange of glance between them. The illustration is a counterpart to the walk in the garden in that Estella still appears haughty and Pip resigned as he walks forward holding his hat in both hands. Interestingly, a top hat has replaced the earlier bowler as if to suggest the advance of both years and maturity. Estella is more sedate and has lost that flamboyant pose of the earlier scene, but she retains the dignity and distance of the former scene. The couple are overshadowed by a weeping willow in the background and they pass between an ornate box-tomb behind them and a more simple gravestone before them. There is a suggestion, perhaps, that their future may be a little like that at the conclusion to *Little Dorrit* where Arthur Clennam and Amy went down 'into a modest life of usefulness and happiness'. Philip V. Allingham, in his invaluable contributions to the role played by the illustrations in *Great Expectations*, suggests that significant departures from correspondence with textual accuracy were rare among Victorian illustrated editions 'because the illustrator was aware of the constraints placed upon artistic license by the presence of the text, and therefore produced plates that complemented the written text rather than undermined it' (Allingham, 'Commentary'). He also points out that the advent of cinema seemed to remove these constraints, and refers to the 1921 silent film where Pip and Estella 'embrace in front of the shattered walls and barred windows of Satis House' (*ibid.*). In similar vein at the end of David Lean's film Pip goes back to Satis House which he finds intact but with a notice outside, 'For Sale'. Like the knight of romance, he enters the main door and climbs up to Miss Havisham's room to find Estella there. Her marriage to Bentley Drummle has been cancelled and she intends to stay amid the dust and relics of her past away from the complications of life. At this point Pip manfully pulls down the curtains and breaks open the shutters which have kept out the light. He turns to Estella and commands her to accompany him into the sunlight to break away from the years of dust and decay and the film ends with them running hand in hand, like happy children released from the ogres of a haunting past. This distortion of Dickens's text leaves the viewer with an uplifted sense of relief that one can indeed escape from the past in order to begin life again.

One of the most dramatic moments of the novel is chapter 53, when Pip answers the summons to attend a meeting on the marshes, and the confrontation with Orlick offers a distinctive opportunity for the illustrator to create an atmosphere of menace and terror. 'On the Marshes, by the Lime-kiln' is one of Marcus Stone's more successful interpretations of mood. The large moon and threatening sky dominate the scene, while the shadowy buildings on the right-hand side of the plate have an air of Gothic gloom. A slightly bowed Pip makes his way towards this building with a sense of inevitability. The mood of the illustration captures something of Dickens's prose:

> There was a melancholy wind, and the marshes were very dismal. A stranger would have found them insupportable, and even to me they were so oppressive that I hesitated, half inclined to go back. But, I knew them well, and could have found my way on a far darker night, and had no excuse for returning, being there. So, having come there against my inclination, I went on against it.

Most illustrators take the confrontation between Pip and Orlick as the subject of their composition, and here Pailthorpe's is startlingly powerful. The demonic Orlick, shorter and lower than the imprisoned Pip, seems to step out of the infernal regions as he holds his flaring candle up to Pip's face. The atmosphere of a trap is skilfully achieved by having the door which is directly behind Orlick bolted with an enormous beam while the ladder to which it is tied seems like a grating which leads up to a black hole in the ceiling. The illustration seems to owe homage to earlier depictions of Dickensian scenes, and Orlick's face could well belong in Cruikshank's menagerie of evil figures. The sheer violence of the scene is caught well by Harry Furniss in his 'Pip in the Power of Dolge Orlick', where the trapped man is held tightly at the mercy of the central figure whose approaching right leg carries with it a momentum of seeming inevitability.

The illustration which emphasizes the psychological connections between the two antagonists is Charles Green's Gadshill Edition plate. Orlick here is close in age to Pip and the two could almost be doubles. With the flaring light between them one could almost imagine the seated Orlick being a version of the working-class Pip holding out the threatening gun against the trussed-up figure of his aspirations. This link between the two characters is also emphasized in H. M. Brock's 1903 illustration where Orlick, a thickly built working man, shines the light on the shadowy prisoner as if to expose the imposter for who he really is. David Lean's film removes Orlick altogether which has the effect of reducing the complexity of the plot, but also of rendering the sudden death of Mrs Joe rather unconvincing. The Julian Amyes version for the BBC (1981) loses much of the atmosphere by having Pip arrive at the marshes in what appears to be broad daylight. The tension is also lost by having the rescue take place after Orlick's gun has misfired, killing himself.

One aspect of the text which Pailthorpe's illustrations capture to a greater extent than any others is the nostalgic sense of a world gone by. In 'Pip leaves the Village' there is a sense of loss as the figure of the exile is caught looking back at the distant church-spire and roofs which nestle within the wooded landscape. The finger-post seems to indicate his way with an air of the angel's flaming sword guarding the pathway back into Eden. Complementing this, the last illustration to the novel deals with Pip's return to 'The old place by the kitchen firelight', where the domesticity excludes the visiting stranger who puts his head round the door as if to peep in on a scene from the past. Joe sits by the fire holding his pipe and with his left hand gently resting on the shoulder of the little boy who looks up at him with trust and affection. Biddy is patiently working on the other side of the fireplace and the cat sitting on the floor between them seems to complete the harmonious composition. This vignette carries with it the impossibility of ever returning to a past which, inevitably, has fled for ever.

The first black-and-white film version of *Great Expectations* was produced in 1917, and the visual quality of the story with its shift from Kentish marshes to a seething London has gripped directors ever since. A black-and-white silent adaptation was directed in 1921 in Denmark by A.W. Sandberg and this has been followed by versions either for the cinema screen or the television throughout the twentieth century (1946, 1959, 1961, 1967, 1974, 1989, 1998). David Lean's Oscar-winning version is probably the most powerfully striking version which has been done. Lean, no great reader of Dickens, had been to see a theatrical performance of *Great Expectations* in 1939 and was immediately struck with the power of the story. In order to capture the imposing atmosphere of the opening he worked with his art director, John Bryan, and his cinematographer, Guy Green, to employ a forced perspective: the brooding church in the opening background, for instance, was only three metres high! Some of the power of the early scene is also obtained by using point-of-view shots: Pip's glancing up at the wildly shaking branches of the spectral trees establishes the audience's sympathy with the isolated boy. Interestingly, the excruciating sound of the trees creaking was formed by the twisting of wet rope that had already been tightly knotted.

In her fascinating short article for *The Dickensian* in 1998, Elham Afnan compares David Lean's film with Billy Wilder's 1950 film, *Sunset Boulevard*. She makes the point early on that a 'good cinematic adaptation is more than a transcription of a novel onto the screen; it is a means of discovering new insights into the themes that inform the original work.' That Wilder had *Great Expectations* in his mind was clear from the outset when the narrator first described the mansion-house in which the ageing movie star, Norma Desmond, lived:

> A neglected house gets an unhappy look – this one had it in spades. It was like that old woman in *Great Expectations*, that Miss Havisham and her rotting wedding dress and her torn veil, taking it out on the world because she'd been given the go-by.

Comparing the ending of David Lean's film, with its melodramatic destruction of the Poe-like hangings which had obscured the room for so long, with the shooting of the narrator, Joe Gillis, as he attempts to leave the mansion in Sunset Boulevard, Elham Afnan points to the director as critic:

> Wilder's film, particularly its ending, is more in keeping with Dickens's preoccupation with entrapment and confinement.

Gillis never manages to leave the decrepit mansion behind. He is engulfed by the luxuries he has sought and drowns in the pool he always wanted. Unlike Lean, Wilder refuses to allow his hero an easy and undeserved release from his chains. Whereas Lean's ending strikes many viewers as a violent switch from realism to melodrama, Wilder's is closer to Dickens's vision in mood and overall tone and is therefore a more palatable, though much looser, interpretation.

In terms of 'discovering new insights into the themes that inform the original work', Alfonso Cuaron's 1998 version of the novel with Ethan Hawke as Pip and Gwyneth Paltrow as Estella is an interesting experiment. The setting of the action has been transposed to Florida and New York and the timing is twentieth-century. Continuing the idea of Pip (Finn as he is called in the film) as narrator, Cuaron allows us to see most of the action through his eyes. Pamela Katz, in her essay on the film for *Dickens on Screen*, points to one of the intriguing aspects of the relationship between Pip and Estella:

> His vision of Estella is particularly stylised. Her face is usually photographed in an extreme (and extremely flattering) close-up: it always appears suddenly, by Finn's side, and then just as suddenly leaves. This surreal touch makes her seem more like a figment of Finn's imagination than a solid human figure. Her reality rests in his mind alone.
>
> (Katz, p. 236)

This offers an interesting comment upon the beautiful girl who, when Pip calls her at Miss Havisham's bidding on his first visit to Satis House, 'answered at last, and her light came along the long dark passage like a star.'

For those who think that interpretation and criticism can be taken too far, Philip V. Allingham's website contribution, '*Great Expectations* in Film and Television, 1917 to 1998', mentions *Southpark*'s Episode No. 62 from November 2000:

> Writer Trey Parker provides a science-fiction treatment of the novel as Malcolm McDowell . . . narrates what begins as a textually accurate synopsis but turns into a fantastic yarn about a

Genesis device on the Havesham Estate designed to emasculate young men . . . Estella is still the main romantic interest, the scornful beauty for whom Pip realizes only a gentleman will do, but her insults have a most un-Dickensian, in-your-face sting. The sitcom departs from the original text significantly, when, after mere months away in London, Pip returns to uncover Miss Havesham's scheme to use his tears and those of other heart-broken young men to enable her Genesis device to ensnare Estella's soul and allow her to live forever while exacting revenge on the entire male gender.

Note: the illustrations to *Great Expectations* referred to in this chapter may all be located on the excellent website which is edited by Philip V. Allingham, Faculty of Education, Lakehead University, Thunder Bay, Ontario (www.victorianweb.org/authors/dickens/ge). The only exception is the Folio edition with the illustrations by Charles Keeping.

STUDY QUESTIONS

1. If you were making a modern film version of *Great Expectations*, would you insist upon it being placed in a nineteenth-century landscape and city world, or could you imagine it being transposed to a twenty-first-century setting? Give clear reasons for your choice, trying to illustrate your argument from what you think the novel is about.
2. If you were writing a stage-adaptation of *Great Expectations*, you would, inevitably, have to leave out a considerable amount of detail. What areas of the plot would you cut and which characters would you remove?
3. The Newgate novel *Oliver Twist* has been made into a highly successful musical despite the grim tone of much of Dickens's writing. If you were going to turn *Great Expectations* into a musical, which qualities of the novel would you have to emphasize and which would you have to play down?

CHAPTER 6

WORKS CITED AND FURTHER READING

EDITIONS OF *GREAT EXPECTATIONS*

Great Expectations, 3 vols, London: Chapman and Hall, 1861.

Great Expectations, London: Chapman and Hall, 1862.

Illustrated Library Edition, with illustrations by Marcus Stone, London: Chapman and Hall, 1864.

The Household Edition, illustrated by F. A. Fraser, London: Chapman and Hall, 1877.

Gadshill Edition, illustrated by Charles Green, London: Chapman and Hall, 1897.

Great Expectations, illustrated by Harry Furniss, London: London Educational Book Company, 1910.

The New Oxford Illustrated Edition, with illustrations by F. W. Pailthorpe, Oxford: Oxford University Press, 1953.

The Folio Society Edition, introduction by Christopher Hibbert and illustrations by Charles Keeping, London: Folio Society, 1981.

Clarendon Dickens, ed. Margaret Cardwell, Oxford: Clarendon Press, 1993.

Great Expectations Case Studies in Contemporary Criticism, ed. Janice Carlisle, Boston, MA: Bedford, 1996.

Oxford World's Classics, ed. Margaret Cardwell, with introduction by Kate Flint, Oxford: Oxford University Press, 1998.

Great Expectations, ed. Charlotte Mitchell, with introduction by David Trotter, Harmondsworth: Penguin Classics, 2003.

OTHER WORKS BY DICKENS

American Notes for General Circulation, Oxford Illustrated Dickens, Oxford: Oxford University Press, 1957.

Barnaby Rudge, Oxford Illustrated Dickens, Oxford: Oxford University Press, 1954.

Bleak House, Oxford Illustrated Dickens, Oxford: Oxford University Press, 1975.

Christmas Books, Oxford Illustrated Dickens, Oxford: Oxford University Press, 1970.

David Copperfield, Oxford Illustrated Dickens, Oxford: Oxford University Press, 1947.

Dombey and Son, Oxford Illustrated Dickens, Oxford: Oxford University Press, 1970.

Hard Times, Oxford Illustrated Dickens, Oxford: Oxford University Press, 1947.

Little Dorrit, Oxford Illustrated Dickens, Oxford: Oxford University Press, 1966.

Martin Chuzzlewit, Oxford Illustrated Dickens, Oxford: Oxford University Press, 1951.

The Mystery of Edwin Drood, Oxford Illustrated Dickens, Oxford: Oxford University Press, 1972.

Nicholas Nickleby, Oxford Illustrated Dickens, Oxford: Oxford University Press, 1966.

The Old Curiosity Shop, Oxford Illustrated Dickens, Oxford: Oxford University Press, 1951.

Oliver Twist, Oxford Illustrated Dickens, Oxford: Oxford University Press, 1968.

Our Mutual Friend, Oxford Illustrated Dickens, Oxford: Oxford University Press, 1952.

The Pickwick Papers, Oxford Illustrated Dickens, Oxford: Oxford University Press, 1949.

Sketches by Boz, Oxford Illustrated Dickens, Oxford: Oxford University Press, 1957.

A Tale of Two Cites, Oxford Illustrated Dickens, Oxford: Oxford University Press, 1960.

The Uncommercial Traveller and Reprinted Pieces, Oxford Illustrated Dickens, Oxford: Oxford University Press, 1958.

WORKS CITED AND FURTHER READING

BIOGRAPHIES, SOCIAL CONTEXTS AND GENERAL STUDIES

Oxford Reader's Companion to Dickens, ed. Paul Schlicke, Oxford: Oxford University Press, 1999.

The Letters of Dickens: Volume 8, 1856–1858, ed. Graham Storey and Kathleen Tillotson, Oxford: Clarendon Press, 1995.

The Letters of Charles Dickens: Volume 9, 1859–1861, ed. Graham Storey, Oxford: Clarendon Press, 1997.

Dickens' Journalism, vol. 3: 'Gone Astray' and Other Papers from 'Household Words', 1851–59, ed. Michael Slater, London: Dent, 1998.

Dickens' Journalism, vol. 4: The Uncommercial Traveller and Other Papers 1859–70, eds Michael Slater and John Drew, London: Dent, 2000.

Ackroyd, Peter, *Dickens*, London: Sinclair-Stevenson, 1990.

Allen, Michael, *Charles Dickens' Childhood*, London: Macmillan, 1988.

Best, Geoffrey, *Mid-Victorian Britain 1851–1875*, New York: Schocken Books, 1972.

Brown, James M., *Dickens: Novelist in the Market-Place: A Sociological Reading*, London: Macmillan, 1982.

Carey, John, *The Violent Effigy: A Study of Dickens's Imagination*, London: Faber, 1973.

Collins, Philip, *Dickens and Crime*, London: Macmillan, 1962.

Collins, Philip (ed.) *Charles Dickens: The Public Readings*, Oxford: Clarendon Press, 1975.

Collins, Wilkie, *The Woman in White*, London: Samson Low, Sons & Co., 1860.

Cook, James, *Bibliography of the Writings of Charles Dickens and Many Curious and Interesting Particulars Relating to His Works*, London: Frank Kerslake,1879.

Egan, Pierce, *Life in London or, the Day and Night Scenes of Jerry Hawthorn, esq. and his elegant friend Corinthian Tom accompanied by Bob Logic, the Oxonian in their Rambles and Sprees through the Metropolis*, London: Sherwood, Neely & Jones, 1821.

Feltes, N. N., *Modes of Production of Victorian Novels*, Chicago, IL: University of Chicago Press, 1986.

Fielding, K. J., *The Speeches of Charles Dickens*, Oxford: Clarendon Press, 1960.

Flint, Kate, *Dickens*, Brighton: Harvester, 1986.

Forster, John, *The Life of Charles Dickens*, 3 vols in 1, London: Chapman and Hall, 1873.

Garis, R., *The Dickens Theatre: A Reassessment of the Novels*, Oxford: Clarendon Press, 1965.

Gilmour, Robin, *The Idea of the Gentleman in the Victorian Novel*, London: Allen and Unwin, 1981.

Gross, John and Gabriel Pearson, *Dickens and the Twentieth Century*, London: Routledge & Kegan Paul, 1962.

Hardy, Barbara, *The Moral Art of Dickens*, London: Athlone Press, 1970.

Hollier, Denis, *Against Architecture: The Writings of George Bataille*, Cambridge, MA/London: The MIT Press, 1989.

House, Humphrey, *The Dickens World*, Oxford: Oxford University Press, 1941.

Hugo, Victor, *The Last Day of a Condemned Man*, trans. Geoff Woollen, London: Hesperus Press, 2002.

Johnson, Edgar, *Charles Dickens: His Tragedy and Triumph*, 2 vols, New York: Simon & Schuster 1952.

Kaplan, Fred, *Dickens: A Biography*, New York: Morrow, 1988.

Lever, Charles, *A Day's Ride*, London: Chapman and Hall, 1863.

Lillo, George, *The London Merchant, or, the History of George Barnwell*, ed. William H. McBurney, Lincoln, NE/London: University of Nebraska Press, 1965.

Lucas, John, *Charles Dickens: The Major Novels*, Harmondsworth: Penguin, 1992.

Mengham, Rod, *Dickens* (Writers and Their Works), Plymouth: Northcote House, 2001.

Morris, Pam, *Dickens's Class Consciousness: A Marginal View*, New York: St Martin's, 1991.

Page, Norman, *A Dickens Chronology*, Boston, MA: G. K. Hall, 1988.

Richards, Thomas, *The Commodity Culture of Victorian England: Advertising and Spectacle 1851–1914*, Stanford, CA: Stanford University Press, 1990.

Schwarzback, F. S., *Dickens and the City*, London: Athlone Press, 1979.

Slater, Michael, *Dickens and Women*, Standford, CA: Stanford University Press, 1983.

Smith, Grahame, *Dickens, Money, and Society*, Berkeley, CA: University of California Press, 1969.

Stone, Harry, *Dickens and the Invisible World: Fairy Tales, Fantasy and Novel-Making*, Bloomington, IN/London: Indiana University Press, 1979.

Stone, Harry (ed.), *Dickens's Working Notes for his Novels*, Chicago, IL: University of Chicago Press, 1987.

Sutherland, J. A., *Victorian Novelists and Publishers*, Chicago, IL: University of Chicago Press, 1976.

Thackeray, W. M., 'Roundabout Papers, No. 8', *Cornhill Magazine*, 1860.

Thompson, F. M. L., *The Rise of Respectable Society: A Social History of Victorian Britain 1830–1900*, Cambridge, MA: Harvard University Press, 1988.

Tomalin, Claire, *The Invisible Woman: The Story of Nelly Ternan and Charles Dickens*, New York: Viking, 1990.

Trilling, Lionel, 'Manners, Morals, and the Novel', in *The Liberal Imagination*, New York: Doubleday Anchor Books, 1950.

Van Ghent, Dorothy, *The English Novel: Form and Function*, New York: Holt, Rinehart and Winston, 1953.

Wilson, Angus, *The World of Charles Dickens*, London: Secker & Warburg, 1970.

INDIVIDUAL PASSAGES

Passage 1: 'Dickens and the Uncanny: Repression and Displacement in *Great Expectations*', *Dickens Studies Annual* 13, 1984.

Passage 2: For a possible source of the figure of Miss Havisham see 'Where We Stopped Growing', *Household Words*, 1 January 1853.

Curt Hartog, 'The Rape of Miss Havisham', *Studies in the Novel* 14, 1982.

Passage 4: Pip's journey from Rochester to London is partly re-written from 'Dullborough Town', *All the Year Round*, 30 June 1860.

Passage 5: In terms of the criminal background for the novel, see 'Five New Points of Criminal Law', *All the Year Round*, 24

September 1859. This short piece deals with the case of Thomas Smethurst who was sentenced to death for the poisoning of a woman whom he had bigamously married. He was later pardoned of the murder. A reference in the 1961 essay, 'The Critical Autonomy of *Great Expectations*' (*Review of English Literature, Vol 2*, p. 27), by K. J. Fielding suggests that Dickens may have had this case in mind when treating Orlick and Mrs Joe.

A reference to the 'spiked' wicket-gate at Newgate and a concern with homeless youths can be found in 'Night Walks', *All the Year Round*, 21 July 1860.

Passage 7: For comments on the gloom and isolation of chambers see 'The Ghost of Art', *Household Words*, 20 July 1850.

Passage 9: Dickens's interest in the Thames Police and a four-oared galley can be seen in 'Down with the Tide', *Household Words*, 5 February 1853.

CRITICAL RECEPTION AND PUBLISHING HISTORY

Axton, William, '*Great Expectations* Yet Again', *Dickens Studies Annual* 2, 1972.

Barnard, Robert, 'Imagery and Theme in *Great Expectations*', *Dickens Studies Annual* 1, 1970.

Baumgarten, Murray, 'Calligraphy and Code: Writing in *Great Expectations*', *Dickens Studies Annual* 11, 1983.

Brooks, Peter, 'Repetition, Repression and Return: The Plotting of *Great Expectations*', in *Reading for the Plot: Design and Intention in Narrative*, Cambridge, MA: Harvard University Press, 1984.

Brown, Carolyn, '*Great Expectations*: Masculinity and Modernity', in *English and Cultural Studies*, ed. Michael Green, London: J. Murray, 1987.

Brown, J. M., *Dickens: Novelist in the Market-Place: A Sociological Reading*, London: Macmillan, 1982.

Buckley, Jerome Hamilton, *Season of Youth: The Bildungsroman from Dickens to Golding*, Cambridge, MA: Harvard University Press, 1974.

Carey, John, *The Violent Effigy: A Study of Dickens's Imagination*, London: Faber, 1973.

Carter, Paul, *The Road to Botany Bay: An Exploration of Landscape and History*, New York: Knopf, 1988.

Cheadle, Brian, 'Sentiment and Resentment in Great Expectations', *Dickens Studies Annual 20*, 1991.

Chorley, H. F., '*Great Expectations*', *Athenaeum*, 13 July 1861.

Cohen, William A., 'Manual Conduct in *Great Expectations*', *ELH* 60, 1993.

Collins, Philip (ed.), *Charles Dickens: The Critical Heritage*, London: Routledge, 1971.

Collins, Philip, 'The Popularity of Dickens', *Dickensian* 70, 1974.

Connolly, Thomas E., 'Technique in *Great Expectations*', *Philological Quarterly* 34, 1955.

Connor, Steven, *Charles Dickens* (Longman's Critical Readers series), London/New York: Longman, 1996.

Cotsell, Michael, *Critical Essays on Charles Dicken's* Great Expectations, Boston, MA: Hall, 1990.

Fielding, K. J., 'The Critical Autonomy of *Great Expectations*', *Review of English Literature* 2, 1961.

Ford, George H., *Dickens and his Readers: Aspects of Novel Criticism since 1836*, Princeton, NJ: Princeton University Press, 1955.

Foucault, Michel, *Discipline and Punish: The Birth of the Prison*, London: Penguin, 1977.

French, A. L., 'Beating and Cringing: *Great Expectations*', *Essays in Criticism* 24, 1974.

Frost, Lucy, 'Taming to Improve: Dickens and the Women in *Great Expectations*', *Meridian* 1, 1982.

Garis, Robert, *The Dickens Theatre*, Oxford: Clarendon Press, 1965.

Gervais, David, 'The Prose and Poetry of *Great Expectations*', *Dickens Studies Annual* 13, 1984.

Gilbert, Elliot L., 'In Primal Sympathy: *Great Expectations* and the Secret Life', *Dickens Studies Annual* 11, 1983.

Gilead, Sarah, 'Barmecide Feasts: Ritual, Narrative, and the Victorian Novel', *Dickens Studies Annual* 17, 1988.

Ginsburg, M. P., 'Dickens and the Uncanny: Repression and Displacement in *Great Expectations*', *Dickens Studies Annual* 13, 1984.

Gissing, George, *Charles Dickens: A Critical Study*, London: Gresham Publishing Co., 1903.

Hagan, John, 'Structural Patterns in Dickens's *Great Expectations*', *ELH: Journal of English Literary History* 21, 1954.

Hara, Eiichi, 'Stories Present and Absent in *Great Expectations*', *English Literary History* 53, 1986.

Hartog, Curt, 'The Rape of Miss Havisham', *Studies in the Novel* 14, 1982.

Hillis Miller, J., *Charles Dickens: The World of his Novels*, Cambridge, MA: Harvard University Press, 1958.

Hurst, Beth F., *The Dickens Hero: Selfhood and Alienation in the Dickens World*, London: Weidenfeld and Nicholson, 1990.

Hutter, Albert, 'Crime and Fantasy in *Great Expectations*', in *Psychoanalysis and the Literary Process*, ed. F. Crews, Cambridge, MA: Harvard University Press, 1970.

Jordan, John O., 'The Medium of *Great Expectations*', *Dickens Studies Annual* 11, 1983.

Kestner, Joseph A., *The Spatiality of the Novel*, Detroit, MI: Wayne State University Press, 1978.

Lang, Andrew, 'Charles Dickens', *Fortnightly Review* 64, 1898.

Leavis, F. R. and Q. D., *Dickens the Novelist*, London: Chatto & Windus, 1970.

Lecker, Barbara, 'The Split Characters of Charles Dickens', *Studies in English Literature 1500–1900* 19, 1979.

Lettis, Richard, *Assessing Great Expectations: Materials for Analysis* San Francisco, CA: Chandler, 1960.

Lewes, G. H., 'Dickens in Relation to Criticism', *Fortnightly Review* 17, 1872.

Litvak, Leon, 'Dickens, Australia and Magwitch: Part 1 – The Colonial Context', *The Dickensian* 95: 1, Spring 1999.

Litvak, Leon, 'Dickens, Australia and Magwitch: Part 2 – The Search for *le cas* Magwitch, *The Dickensian* 95: 2, Summer 1999.

Lohman, W. J., 'The Economic Background of *Great Expectations*', *Victorians Institute Journal* 14, 1986.

McMaster, Rowland and Juliet, *The Novel from Sterne to James: Essays in the Relation of Literature to Life*, London: Macmillan, 1981.

Marlow, James E., 'English Cannibalism: Dickens after 1859', *SEL* 23, 1983.

Meckier, Jerome, 'Dating the Action in *Great Expectations*: A New Chronology', *Dickens Studies Annual* 21, 1992.

Meckier, Jerome, 'Charles Dickens's *Great Expectations*: A Defense of the Second Ending', *Studies in the Novel* 25, 1993.

Morris, Christopher D., 'The Bad Faith of Pip's Bad Faith: Deconstructing *Great Expectations*', *English Literary History* 54, 1987.

Morris, Mowbray, 'Charles Dickens', *Fortnightly Review* 32, 1882.

Morris, Pam, '*Great Expectations*: A Bought Self', in *Dickens's Class Consciousness: A Marginal View*, New York: St Martin's, 1991.

Moynahan, Julian, 'The Hero's Guilt: the Case of *Great Expectations*', *Essays in Criticism* 10, January 1960.

Newton, Judith, 'Historicism Old and New: Charles Dickens Meets Marxism, Feminism, and West Coast Foucault', *Feminist Studies* 16, 1990.

Oliphant, Margaret, 'Sensation Novels', *Blackwood's Edinburgh Magazine* 91, May 1862.

Orwell, George, 'Charles Dickens', *The Collected Essays, Journalism and Letters of George Orwell, Vol. 1*, London: Secker & Warburg, 1968.

Paroissien, David, *The Companion to Great Expectations*, Mountfield: Helm, 2000.

Rawlins, Jack, 'Great Expiations: Dickens and the Betrayal of the Child', *Studies in English Literature 1500–1900* 23, 1983.

Ron, Moshe, 'Autobiographical Narration and Formal Closure in *Great Expectations*', *Hebrew University Studies in Literature* 5, 1977.

Rosenberg, Edgar, 'Last Words on *Great Expectations*: A Textual Brief on the Six Endings', *Dickens Studies Annual* 9, 1981.

Sadrin, Anny, *Great Expectations*, London: Unwin Hyman, 1988.

Schor, Hilary, 'If He Should Turn to and Beat Her': Violence, Desire, and the Woman's Story in *Great Expectations*', in *Great Expectations: Case Studies in Contemporary Criticism*, ed. Janice Carlisle, Boston, MA: Bedford, 1996, pp. 541–57.

Schwarzback, F. S., *Dickens and the City*, London, 1979.

Sell, Roger D., *Great Expectations* (New Casebook series), New York: Macmillan, 1994.

Siegal, Carol, 'Postmodern Women Novelists Review Victorian Male Masochism', *Genders* 11, 1991.

Swinburne, A. C., 'Charles Dickens', *Quarterly Review*, July 1902.

Tambling, Jeremy, 'Prison-Bound: Dickens, Foucault and *Great Expectations*', in *Dickens, Violence and the Modern State*, London: Macmillan, 1995.

Wall, Stephen (ed.), *Charles Dickens: A Critical Anthology*, London: Penguin, 1970.

Walsh, Susan, 'Bodies of Capital: *Great Expectations* and the Climacteric Economy', *Victorian Studies* 37, 1993.

Watt, Ian, 'Oral Dickens', *Dickens Studies Annual* 3, 1974.

Whipple, Edwin P., 'Dicken's Great Expectations', *The Atlantic Monthly* 8 September 1861, pp. 380–2.

Wilson, Edmund, *The Wound and the Bow*, Boston, MA: Houghton Mifflin, 1941.

Worth, George J., *Great Expectations: An Annotated Bibliography*, New York 1986.

ADAPTATION, INTERPRETATION AND INFLUENCE

Afnan, Elham, 'Imaginative Transformations: *Great Expectations* and *Sunset Boulevard*', *The Dickensian* 94: 1, Spring 1998.

Allingham, Philip V., 'Commentary' to 'Estella and Pip', The Victorian Web, www.victorianweb.org/art/illustration/furniss/461.html (accessed November 2006).

Allingham, Philip V., '*Great Expectations* in Film and Television, 1917 to 1998', The Victorian Web, www.victorianweb.org/authors/dickens/ge/filmadapt.html (accessed November 2006).

Browne, Edgar, *Phiz and Dickens As They Appeared to Edgar Browne*, London: James Nisbet, 1913.

Buchanan-Brown, John, *Phiz! The Book Illustrations of Hablot Knight Browne*, Newton Abbot: David & Charles, 1978.

Davis, Paul B., 'Dickens, Hogarth, and the Illustrated *Great Expectations*', *The Dickensian* 80: 3, Autumn 1984.

DeBona, Guerric, 'Doing Time; Undoing Time: Plot Mutation in David Lean's *Great Expectations*', *Literature/Film Quarterly* 20, 1992.

Eisenstein, Sergei, 'Dickens, Griffith, and the Film Today', in *Film Form: Essays in Film Theory*, ed. Jan Leyda, New York: Harcourt Brack, 1949.

Giddings, Robert, 'Great Misrepresentations: Dickens and Film', *Critical Survey* 3, 1991.

Giddings, Robert, 'Review of BBC2's *Great Expectations*', *The Dickensian* 95: 2, Summer 1999.

Great Expectations (film), dir. A. W. Sandberg, Denmark, 1921.

Great Expectations (film), dir. David Lean, 1947.

Great Expectations (TV), dir. Julian Aymes, BBC, 1981.

Great Expectations (film), dir. Alfonso Cuaron, 1998.

Hammerton, J. A., *The Dickens Picture-Book*, London: Educational Book Co., n. d. [1910?].

Harvey, J. R., *Victorian Novelists and their Illustrators*, London: Sidgwick & Jackson, 1970.

James, Henry, *The Bench of Desolation*, Whitefish, MT: Kessinger Publishing Co., 2004,

James, P., *English Book Illustration 1800–1900*, London: Penguin Books, 1947.

Johannsen, Albert, *Phiz: Illustrations from the Novels of Charles Dickens*, Chicago, IL: University of Chicago Press, 1956.

Katz, Pamela, 'Directing Dickens: Alfonso Cuaron's 1998 *Great Expectations*', in *Dickens on Screen*, ed. J. Glavin, Cambridge: Cambridge University Press, 2003.

Kitton, F. G., *Dickens and his Illustrators*, London: George Redway, 1899.

Lester, Valerie Browne, *Phiz: The Man Who Drew Dickens*, London: Chatto and Windus, 2004.

McFarlane, Brian, 'David Lean's *Great Expectations*: Meeting Two Challenges', *Literature/Film Quarterly* 20, 1992.

MacKay, Carol Hanbery, 'A Novel's Journey into Film: The Case of *Great Expectations*', *Literature/Film Quarterly* 13, 1985.

Mayhew, Henry, *London Labour and the London Poor, volume 1*, London: Griffin, Bohn, and Company, 1861.

Meisel, Martin, *Realizations: Narrative, Pictorial, and Theatrical Arts in Nineteenth-Century England*, Princeton, NJ: Princeton University Press, 1983.

Moynahan, Julian, 'Seeing the Book, Reading the Movie', in *The English Novel and the Movies*, ed. Michael Klein and Gillian Parker, New York: Ungar, 1981.

Muir, Percy, *Victorian Illustrated Books*, London: Batsford, 1971.

Reid, F., *Illustrators of the Sixties*, London: Faber & Gwyer, 1928.

Sinyard, Neil, *Filming Literature: The Art of Screen Adaptation*, London: Croon Helm, 1986.

Solberg, Sarah A., 'A Note on Phiz's Dark Plates', *Dickensian* 76: 1, Spring 1980.

Steig, Michael, *Dickens and Phiz*, Bloomington, IN/London: Indiana University Press, 1978.

Sunset Boulevard (film), dir. Billy Wilder, 1950.

Tharaud, Barry, '*Great Expectations* as Literature and Film', *The Dickensian* 87: 1, Spring 1991.

Watts, Alan S., 'Why Wasn't *Great Expectations* Illustrated?', *The Dickens Magazine* 1: 2, 2001.

White, G., *English Illustration 'The Sixties': 1855–1870*, London: Archibald Constable & Co., 1897.

INDEX

INDEX